Culinary Arts Institute®

COOKING with
BEER

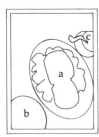

Featured in cover photo:
a. **German Pork Roast in Spicy Beer Sauce** 29
b. **Sweet-Sour Red Cabbage** 29
c. **Easy Beer-Cheese Soup** 27

COOKING with BEER

COOKING WITH BEER

Annette Ashlock Stover
and The Culinary Arts Institute Staff
Edward G. Finnegan, Executive Editor
Book Designed and Coordinated by Charles Bozett
Illustrations by Seymour Fleishman
Photos by Zdenek Pivecka

Culinary Arts Institute®
A DIVISION OF DELAIR/CONSOLIDATED   new york

CONTENTS

The Story of Beer 7
The Art of Serving Beer 11
Using Beer in the Kitchen 13

Glossary 14

Menus 15
  Smorgasbord 16
  Winter Chili Supper 18
  St. Patrick's Day Dinner 20
  Backyard Beer Bash 23
  Mexican Fiesta Party 24
  Tailgate Football Picnic 26
  Oktoberfest Dinner Party 28
  Holiday Open House 31

Appetizers 33

Breads 37

Soups 43

Cheese and Eggs 49

Meat 55

Poultry and Fish 65

Sauces and Dressings 71

Vegetables and Salads 77

Desserts 83

Beverages 91

Index 94

The STORY of BEER

Beer—that bubbling, thirst-quenching, piquantly bitter brew—has been delighting people around the world for thousands of years. It has truly been the drink of "the common man." Only tea now outranks it in total volume consumed. Twice as much beer is drunk as wine, and through the centuries beer has usually been more readily available and affordable than wine for the average person.

Historians are not sure when beer was first made, but they do know it was one of the earliest of alcoholic beverages. Fermented grain (beer), fermented honey (mead), and fermented fruit juice (wine) all go back to an era prior to recorded history. The first beer probably was created quite by accident. A jar of mashed grain and water got set aside, natural yeasts from the air began acting upon it, and later someone tasted the unusual liquid—much to his delight.

Beer is mentioned on some of the oldest tablets of written history yet found. It was one of the provisions on Noah's Ark, according to an Assyrian tablet found in Nineveh. A Babylonian tablet six thousand years old depicts two men stirring the contents of a brewery vat. Babylon and Nineveh were the principal cities of ancient Mesopotamia in the valleys of the Tigris and Euphrates rivers, now in Iraq.

Even in preagricultural times, nine thousand years ago and more, beer was enjoyed. Some historians speculate that the formal agricultural system characteristic of the New Stone Age, especially the planting of grains, may have sprung from the desire to always have on hand the ingredients for making beer.

Interestingly, most of the ancient peoples of the world made some kind of beer. The Babylonians, Assyrians, and Egyptians perfected brewing and raised it to a high art, but the Chinese, Incas, various African tribes, Hebrews, Teutons, Saxons, and East European peoples all enjoyed beer.

Religious significance was placed upon beer by several of the ancient civilizations. Beer is not mentioned in the Bible, but references to wine probably included beer, for wine was then a broad term covering all fermented beverages. The Babylonians designated the goddesses Ninkasi and Siris to watch over their beer. Anu, god of the sky, was accustomed to receiving offerings of four special beers in the Temple of Uruk, according to records dating back 5,400 years.

In Egypt, beer was regularly offered to the gods. Ramses III is known to have sacrificed thirty thousand gallons yearly from his royal brewery. When mummies were placed in their tombs a supply of beer was left, along with various riches, for consumption in the afterworld. The Egyptians also had a goddess of brewing called Isis.

Everyone in Egypt apparently drank beer. Royalty and the upper classes produced fine beers in private brewhouses. They also sipped beer through golden straws, as did the rich of Mesopotamia. Ordinary people gathered at House of Beer establishments to drink a more common brew. Even children went to school with bread and jugs of beer. A 1600 B.C. medical text lists beer in one hundred of seven hundred prescriptions in use at that time.

Women were the brewers in both ancient Mesopotamia and Egypt, and they also were the temple beer priestesses. Later, through the growth of a type of brewers' craft union and by decree of

King Hammurabi, men became master brewers, while women continued to operate the taverns and performed lesser tasks of mashing and stirring.

The early beers would certainly not please palates of today. Although many types were made, most were cloudy and flat. Beer was served without chilling, and it was not made with hops to give the characteristic, slightly bitter taste. Instead, flavorings included eggshells, oyster shells, crab claws, wormwood seeds, horehound juice, and various herbs.

Brewing methods were, of course, quite primitive compared to modern breweries, with their vast metal tanks, miles of pipes, temperature controls, and other fancy equipment. However, the basic principles are remarkably similar.

The major breakthrough for beer brewing for all time came when malting was discovered. Barley, the grain from which beer is made, was watered to swell the grains and germinate them as if they were going to grow. This produced substances which could convert the grain starch to sugar. When dried, this product was called barley malt. It could be stored and was easier to crush than the original grain.

Later the barley malt (and sometimes other grains) was ground and mixed with hot water in large clay vessels in a process called "mashing." The starch quickly converted to sugar dissolved in a brown liquid called "wort." The wort was boiled with flavorings; then the brew was cooled in cellars and a special yeast added. Yeast causes sugar to ferment, yielding alcohol and carbon dioxide. This resulting liquid was the beer.

In ancient times, especially in Egypt, the malt was baked into flat cakes. These could be transported by the armies for brewing an instant beer out in the hinterlands—a pleasant convenience.

The Greeks and Romans knew about brewing beer, but generally preferred wine. Their climate and land were more suitable for growing grapes rather than fields of barley. However, beer was drunk by the soldiers of the Roman army and was probably enjoyed by the common people.

Beer has been brewed in England for at least two thousand years or more. Germanic tribes were brewing beer at the time of Christ or earlier, too. Beer was made all across Eastern and Northern Europe, Gaul (France), Spain, and Scandinavia.

In medieval Europe and England it was generally the monks who were the official brewers of their communities. Beer was also brewed at home by women, but it became such an important source of revenue to the monasteries that in some areas the people were forbidden to brew their own until the monastery supply was exhausted—which seldom happened.

As in former eras, medieval beer was a very common drink because the safety of the water was questionable. Brewing produced a beverage free of disease-causing organisms. At the same time, though, regulations proliferated because too much beer loosened inhibitions and produced public drunkenness. Nevertheless, massive quantities of beer were consumed on a daily basis; even children had it with meals. English monasteries permitted a mere one gallon of good ale and one gallon of weak ale per day for each monk.

Monasteries in England set up hospices around the eighth century which provided overnight accommodations for travelers, including ale and food. Public alehouses featured beer brewed by women known as "alewives."

At that time, ale was simply the English word for beer. Centuries later, when German-style beer was flavored with hops and lagered (aged), ale became different from beer. Now ale is flavored with hops, but a different type of yeast, a top-fermenting one, gives ale a distinctive, stronger flavor than most modern beer.

King Henry II levied the first English tax on ale in 1188; it was formerly considered a food. He taxed other consumer items, too, and used the proceeds to fight the Crusades. Henry III fixed ale prices, with public flogging the punishment for selling watered ale. When the new brew was ready, alehouses had to set out ale stakes or long poles, so that the "ale conner" or taster could come and test for strength and accuracy of measures.

When we think of a typical beer taste today, it is a characteristic bitterness that we expect, a taste given beer by the dried flowers of the hop plant. Beer was not always flavored this way, however. Hops are first believed to have been used in Babylon around A.D. 200. With the great folk migrations following the fall of the Roman Empire, knowledge of delicious hopped beer gradually moved north into areas that are now Bulgaria and Yugoslavia, and later into Bohemia, Germany, and France. In the eighth century A.D., the German Hallertau district had a famous hop garden, as did French royalty.

However, the use of hops was not common and, in fact, was resisted almost everywhere. Most beer in Europe was flavored with *gruit,* a secret blend of ingredients often controlled by powerful political interests, usually the Church. The gruit makers did not want to lose their monopoly.

Areas like Hamburg, which did make hopped beer, found their product so prized that an export market grew. Finally in the thirteenth century, hopped beer became more widespread among the many German beer-producing cities. In England, its use came centuries later, with the first hop garden planted during the reign of Henry VIII.

Another German practice that revolutionized brewing was that of lagering or aging beer instead of selling it immediately. This gave beer a subtle, more sophisticated flavor. Lager beer also used a yeast that settled to the bottom, as opposed to ale yeast, which floated. Most American beer is lager.

In the nineteenth century the city of Pilsen in Bohemia became a famous brewing center because it produced a lovely, light golden beer known as Pilsner or Bohemian beer. Other beer was then darker and heavier, with a more robust aroma.

When Columbus landed in the Caribbean Islands, he found the natives making a "first-rate brew of maize, resembling English beer." In the New World, as in medieval Europe (except for monastery beer), brewing was the responsibility of women.

Beer came to our country with the earliest settlers, since water became undrinkable on the long voyage across the Atlantic. The Pilgrims might have sailed on to Virginia, but they were running out of provisions. A journal of the voyage records: "We could not now take time for further search . . . our victuals being much spente, especially our beer."

America's first "help wanted" advertisement appeared in London in 1609, calling for brewers to serve in Virginia. It was answered by two Frenchmen. One of the first American breweries was established in 1612 in New Amsterdam as sort of a do-it-yourself project where settlers could make their own beer. In 1637, New Amsterdam granted the exclusive right to maintain a brewery to Captain Robert Sedgwick; soon the price rose from one penny a quart to twopence.

Beer was on colonial American tables as regularly as bread, a habit brought from England. A brewhouse was essential to every settlement, and more prosperous households had their own. William Penn, Samuel Adams, Thomas Jefferson, and George Washington were among those making beer.

Beer brewed at home was called "small beer," as distinguished from the professional brewer's product, "strong beer." Many of the colonies, wanting to encourage a local brewing industry, placed duties on imported beer. But beer of that era was a heavy, not-too-subtle beverage, for lagering and hops flavoring were brewing arts not yet brought to this country.

While the English gave our country its thirst for beer, it was the nineteenth-century German immigrants who introduced the fine brewing techniques which set the stage for production of modern American beer.

Hops were grown in America by the time of the Revolutionary War, but it was not until 1840 that the first lager beer was produced. A German immigrant named Wagner brought to Philadelphia some of the special yeast that was needed, and he was familiar with the fine German brewing techniques. As the yeast grew, he was able to increase production. But in addition, a great tide of German immigration swept our shores, and with it came brewmasters, lager beer, and neighborhood beer gardens.

Scientific discoveries changed beer production, too. Louis Pasteur's pasteurization process made beer bottling commercially feasible. Beer formerly was made in the fall and spring, when the temperature was just right. But air conditioning and refrigeration made it possible to brew beer the year round. Controlled fermentation gave beer a consistency of flavor and character. New canning technology brought us beer in cans.

One major setback to beer brewing was the thirteen years of Prohibition in the United States. Brewers struggled for survival, producing "near beer," soft drinks, and even food products. Many went out of business. Illegal bootleg beer spawned an era of underworld crime.

With the repeal of Prohibition in 1933, beer was back to enjoy; but repeal also brought many new government regulations for the sale of beer, wine, and liquor. Gone was the wild heyday of the saloon, and soon Americans were drinking more bottled beer at home than draught beer in taverns.

Today, Americans drink about twenty-two gallons of beer per capita each year, and we are somewhere around eleventh among beer-consuming countries. Czechoslovakia leads the world in per capita consumption, followed by Germany.

But the United States does produce the largest total quantity of beer, followed by West Germany, England, Russia, Japan, Czechoslovakia, France (the Alsace region primarily), Canada, East Germany, Australia, Mexico, Belgium, Spain, Poland, Brazil, Colombia, Austria, the Netherlands, Denmark, Yugoslavia, and Italy.

Beer does contribute a little nutritional value other than calories, unlike hard liquor. A 12-ounce serving contains 1 gram of protein, 18 mg. of calcium, 2.2 mg. niacin (13% of an adult man's daily requirement, 17% of a woman's), and .11 mg. riboflavin (6.5% of a man's daily requirement, 7.3% of a woman's). The caloric value of 12 ounces regular American beer is about 150, more for dark beer, less for light beers.

Much of the beer in the United States is produced by giant breweries, certainly a far cry from the primitive methods of the Egyptians, the medieval monasteries, or even nineteenth-century Germany. Modern breweries use top-grade grains, pure water, exact temperatures at various stages, precise timing, tight control of yeast action, clinic-clean apparatus, immense vats several stories high, cooling systems, miles of pipes, and all kinds of other equipment.

In a small nutshell, here is how beer is brewed today. Compared to Egyptian and Mesopotamian brewing, the equipment is entirely different, but some of the basic principles remain the same.

First barley malt is mashed with hot water, while other grain adjuncts (usually corn or rice) are heating with water in a cooker to gelatinize the starch.

Mash and the other cereals are mixed and heated, converting starch to sugar. The liquid is strained to remove spent grain solids, leaving an amber liquid called "wort."

Next the wort is boiled in giant brew kettles with hops or hops extract, which gives beer its typical flavor. Then the hops are removed and the mixture cooled to about 50°F by flowing it over cooling towers. A special pure beer yeast is added and fermentation begins, converting the sugar to alcohol and carbon dioxide. Often the carbon dioxide is drawn off, converted to liquid, then added later to carbonate or provide bubbles for the beer. Some breweries carbonate beer by kraeusening (see Glossary).

After fermentation, at just the right point the yeast is drawn off and the beer is filtered and piped to giant lagering tanks for aging. Because yeast expands, there are plenty of active cells left to be used for the next batch; every brewery has its prized yeast strain. After aging, the beer is carbonated and placed in barrels, bottles, or cans. The bottles and cans are pasteurized quickly at about 140°F to retard micro-organisms which would harm the beer before it finally reaches the consumer; draught beer is not pasteurized because it is sold and drunk much sooner.

The large modern breweries know what beer is popular with Americans—typically a rather light,

clear, quite sparkling beverage. Extra-light beers are rather new on the market, and some hearty dark beer is brewed. Some of the small breweries continue to follow some old-fashioned techniques to achieve a more European flavor. Also, many foreign beers are imported into this country, and these often use contrasting brewing methods.

Thus, American consumers have a wide gamut of beers from which to choose to suit tastes and pocketbooks. There is a delicious, pleasing beer for everyone. The thing to do is to experiment with many brands to find the one you like best.

The ART of SERVING BEER

A bottle, can, or keg of beer is a delicate, balanced product of the brewer's expertise; it is not an indestructible liquid to be stored indefinitely or handled with abandon. Serving beer at its peak of perfection to guests or to yourself requires a certain degree of care, from the moment of purchase to the pouring and presentation.

When you bring your beer home from the store, it doesn't help the beer to let it sit for several hours in a hot automobile. Hurry it home, especially if the weather is very hot or below freezing. Great changes in temperature can harm the flavor, and, of course, you do not want to run the risk of freezing the beer. Keep it out of the sunlight, too.

A cool, dark place away from light is best for storing beer that you prefer not to refrigerate right away. This helps protect the flavor, body, and strength. Too much light can harm beer in bottles, and too warm a storage temperature is not good for any beer.

In fact, it is really not good to store beer for long periods. Unlike wine, beer does not improve with age, so buy only what you can use relatively soon —even though most bottled and canned beers are pasteurized.

Also unlike wine, beer should be stored upright. There are two reasons for this advice. One is that it minimizes the surface area exposed to air inside the bottle or can. Secondly, it lessens the amount of jostling the beer receives. Most beer drinkers can recognize a bottle or can of beer harmed by too much shaking. Pressure builds inside and the beer foams over when opened, leaving fewer bubbles in the beer to enjoy while drinking.

TEMPERATURE FOR SERVING

Most Americans prefer beer chilled to 40 to 42 degrees Fahrenheit (or to 5 degrees Celsius). This is about the temperature a properly working refrigerator will create. Other countries, England in particular, drink their beer warmer, though not really warm, as some claim. It is more a cold-room temperature. The English claim their full-bodied ales and beers are most flavorful this way. But given the lighter American beers and American temperature preferences, the beer you serve will be more appreciated if served quite cold.

One common chilling practice should really be discouraged: that is the habit of putting warm beer into the freezer to give it a quick chill. You are more likely to harm your sensitive beer, rather than bring it to the ideal serving point you are desiring.

Putting beer in the freezer creates the danger of freezing all or part of the beer. When this happens the beer is likely to become cloudy and lose part of its fine balance of flavor and bouquet. It also may become partially flat. If all the beer freezes, the can or bottle may burst.

A much better plan for quick chilling is to get a large tub or bucket. Place the bottles or cans in it and cover them with ice. Then pour water over the ice. Water conducts the chill to the beer more rapidly than plain ice. Never pour salt over the ice, for this may cause the beer to freeze.

DRINKING VESSELS

For casual refreshment, many people drink beer right from the can or bottle. But that doesn't give you the chance to enjoy the foamy "head" on a glass of fine, well-poured beer or to view the sparkling, clear beverage you are drinking. It's also a bit more civilized to pour beer into a glass or mug when serving guests.

Beer has been served in almost every kind of vessel imaginable. Among the earliest were those hollowed out of stone and vessels made of hides and skins. The old Latin word for bottle was understood to mean a container made of leather. Clay vessels were also made in early times. In ancient Egypt, Greece, and Rome, beverages were drunk from glass, but usually only by the upper classes and royalty.

Much later the Venetians created fine glass goblets and the English devised a number of unusually shaped wood, leather, and metal containers. The Germans have been making fancy ceramic steins for nearly five hundred years.

Today beer is enjoyed in something as simple as a paper cup at a picnic (it should be large enough for the foam and plastic coated to avoid a paper taste) or as elegant as a crystal goblet. Other popular vessels include the tall Pilsner glass, which tapers outward from bottom to top; the glass schooner, a heavy stemmed goblet; the straight-sided small "shell" glass; the rather large "hourglass," which nips in at the middle; and mugs made out of pewter, ceramic material, or heavy glass. Elegantly adorned German beer steins with lids are still used, but many have become collector's items and museum pieces.

Whatever the container you choose for drinking beer, it should be sparkling clean in order to acquire the proper beer foam and preserve the best flavor. You don't want any grease, soap, or lint on the inside. If washed properly, there will be no bubbles clinging to the side of the glass, and the foam will adhere to the inside in a ring design.

Use a soap-free, odorless cleaning agent or a detergent. Baking soda is excellent, too. While you sometimes hear the advice "Don't use soap on beer glasses," what is really meant is not to use a true soap, which can leave a film. The liquid "soaps" on the market are actually detergents and are all right to use. Always rinse beer glasses or mugs very well in clean, cool, running water. Air-drying them avoids any bits of lint which could remain from a towel.

POURING BEER

There's an art to pouring beer, too. Some people like a high, foamy head; others a short one. Beer connoisseurs claim that a head is essential for fullest enjoyment of the brewer's product. But if you want to avoid the head, tilt the glass, then pour in the beer very slowly against the side.

A thick, creamy head can be achieved by letting the beer splash into the glass. A good way to get a moderate head is to tilt the glass and begin pouring the beer down the side; then straighten the glass and pour into the center. You will soon learn how to build a high or low head by varying the distance between the can or bottle and the glass.

In drawing draught beer, the foam should rise to just above the lip of the glass without flowing over. As it settles, there should be three fourths to one inch of foam. If there is too little pressure or the beer is too cold, it may draw with too little foam.

HOW MUCH TO BUY

How much beer should you allow for a party? If you are having a backyard bash or casual indoor party where the beer is the featured attraction, you will probably average four twelve-ounce portions per person (five for men, three for women). If people are just dropping by for an hour or so, figure about two twelve-ounce portions per person.

If the beer is a beverage to be served before and during a dinner party, with a switch to coffee later, two to three twelve-ounce servings will be your likely average.

If you are serving draught beer from a keg, it is helpful to know that a half-barrel keg holds 15½ gallons, a quarter-barrel keg 7¾ gallons. If you are using twelve-ounce glasses or paper cups, about one hundred servings can be poured from a quarter barrel, two hundred from a half barrel. This figure allows for one inch of foam on the top. With more foam, obviously you will pour more glasses. A half-barrel keg yields two hundred servings. Hence, if you plan a beer party for fifty people, you will need a half-barrel keg to average four servings per person.

Tapping equipment is available at the location where you purchase your keg or kegs of beer. Be sure you receive complete instructions on how to use it. It is really quite simple, so draught beer should be considered for a large party. It makes the atmosphere more festive, and it is fun to pour beer from the spigot. Kegs are especially nice for outdoor parties; inside they can get a bit messy.

Keep the keg or kegs in the shade, and on hot days you probably will want to set the tapped keg in a large tub of ice.

USING BEER in the KITCHEN

Beer is so satisfying as a cooling beverage that many people are unaware of its great potential as a flavoring agent in cooking. Although records of its earliest culinary use are unavailable, surely cooks of ancient times poured a bit of their stale home brew into the soup or stewpot to perk up the meal.

Beer is used in cooking in many countries, especially those that brew and consume significant quantities of beer. Several of the great classic recipes of the world call for beer: Welsh Rabbit, the Belgian beef dish known as Carbonnade à la Flamandes, German-style sausages in beer, shrimp boiled in beer, beer soups, beer batters, and German carp in a gingery beer sauce.

This cookbook offers these recipes, plus dozens more. Flip through the pages and you will gain a quick perspective on the wide gamut of intriguing dishes that can be made with beer, from appetizers through entrées, vegetables, breads, and desserts.

From the simplest of dishes to gourmet specialties, beer can change and enhance foods in many ways. Sometimes just a subtle essence remains, as with slowly cooked meat dishes. At other times the beer flavor is more pronounced, as when beer is added to sauces and other dishes at the end of the cooking time.

In baked goods, the flavor may be just barely perceptible or entirely gone, but a lightness and tenderness is given to the end product. Surprisingly delicious results occur when beer goes into sweet desserts. The beer flavor is there, but it is transformed into mellow goodness by the sugar, spices, eggs, and other ingredients.

Beer can be used with assurance in family meals, as well as in adult party dishes, for the alcohol evaporates within the first few minutes of cooking.

Even in uncooked dishes, each person only gets a small quantity of the beer, and it is such a mildly alcoholic beverage—less than 6%.

Here are a number of pointers to help you in using beer in the kitchen:

● The common twelve-ounce bottle or can of beer measures 1½ cups liquid. Many recipes in this book have been designed to use exactly one or two cans of beer to eliminate any problem of leftovers.

● If the recipe calls for less than one can of beer and the beer you are using is cold, you have the delightful option of drinking the extra as a cook's treat or saving it for another recipe.

● It does not matter if the beer is freshly opened or stale. If a specific measure is needed (*i.e.,* less than an even can) and the beer is just opened, pour it a few minutes in advance. This allows the head or foam to settle, permitting a more accurate measurement.

● Beer may be used warm or cold. The cold beer will obviously take a little longer to heat to simmering or boiling.

● Don't throw away portions of unconsumed beer in bottles or cans. Store in the refrigerator in a covered jar for use later in cooking.

● Even small amounts of beer can spark sauces, soups, dressings, and pan gravies.

● Experiment with beer as all or part of the liquid in packaged mixes or in reconstituting instant or freeze-dried foods.

● The longer a beer dish cooks, the less of the characteristic beer flavor remains. If a sauce seems a bit too strong of beer, just simmer it a few minutes longer. Likewise, if you can't taste the beer at all, add a little beer at the end of the cooking period.

GLOSSARY

Alcohol—A colorless liquid (C_2H_5OH) that is the stimulant in fermented beverages and distilled liquors. In beer, the alcoholic content is generally 3% to 6%.

Ale—A type of beer popular in England. Formerly it differed because ale was not flavored with hops. Hops are now put into ale, but it uses a different yeast—a top-fermenting yeast—which adds a more pronounced flavor.

Barley—The major grain from which most beer has been made down through the ages.

Beer—A fermented, alcoholic beverage brewed from barley malt and other grains, plus flavorings and yeast. The malt converts to sugar and the yeast acts upon it to produce alcohol and carbon dioxide.

Bock beer—A special beer usually prepared for early spring consumption. It is darker and richer than regular beer and is made with a caramel malt. It is *not* made from the dregs at the bottom of beer vats, as is sometimes claimed.

Brewer's yeast—An inactive yeast rich in B vitamins and protein used as a food supplement for animals and humans. It is the excess yeast which results after beer fermentation. The more vigorous yeast cells are saved for the next brewing.

Bung—Plug used for closing the hole in a keg.

Carbon dioxide—The gas which creates the bubbles in beer. It is a product of the chemical action of yeast and sugar. In modern breweries, it is usually drawn off, condensed into liquid, and added later, to produce carbonation.

Cooker—A vessel for boiling the unmalted cereal adjuncts (usually corn or rice) to gelatinize the starch. Mash (ground malt and water) is added and the whole cooked to convert starch to sugar.

Draught beer—Beer put into barrels or kegs, usually unpasteurized, for serving through a tap. Most common for tavern use.

Fermentation—The step in beer production when the sugar liquid (wort) and yeast act to produce alcohol and carbon dioxide.

Head—The foam on top of beer after pouring.

Hogshead—A large wooden barrel or cask usually holding more than sixty gallons. Obsolete today.

Hops—The flavoring agent in beer; from a plant related to the mulberry which bears flowers in cone-shaped clusters. When dried, these flowers are used to give the characteristic piquant-bitter flavor to beer. Hop extract is increasingly being used in modern brewing.

Keg—A small barrel for beer, usually containing a quarter-barrel quantity (7¾ gallons) or a half-barrel amount (15½ gallons).

Kraeusening—The addition of a smaller portion of beer or wort in the early stages of fermentation to a larger portion of fermented beer to produce an after-fermentation. Thus the beer is naturally carbonated.

Lager—A beer produced by a German technique which requires storing, rather than drinking immediately. Most U.S. beer is lager. Lager beer is also made with a bottom-fermenting yeast. The flavor of lager is more mellow and sparkling. In contrast, English-style beers and ales are not lagered.

Malt—Grain (usually barley) which has been steeped in water to germinate, then dried. It more easily converts to sugar and is the basic ingredient of beer. Malting has been practiced by brewers for thousands of years.

Malt liquor—A rather new type of beer that is higher in alcohol and lacks the hops taste of lager beer. Its processing is different from regular beer, and its flavor is somewhat like British ale.

Mashing—A step in the early stages of beer production whereby the malt is ground and heated with water.

Pasteurization—Partial sterilization of a liquid at a temperature which destroys or inhibits microorganisms. Bottled and canned beer is pasteurized because it will not be drunk as quickly as draught beer in barrels, which is not pasteurized.

Pilsner—A light, tart, golden type of beer which originated in the Bohemian city of Pilsen.

Porter—A variation of ale with a sweeter, less "hoppy" taste. It is darker, made with several kinds of malt, and is similar to a mixture of old-fashioned ale and weak or "small" beer. Its popularity has waned.

Small beer—A name given in England and colonial American times to weak beer, usually produced at home.

Stout—Very dark, strong, heavy beer especially popular in Ireland.

Strong beer—Old English term for beer of standard strength brewed by professional brewers.

Wort—Liquid obtained from steeping malt in hot water. The starch has converted to sugar and the spent grains have been filtered out, but it is not yet beer until it undergoes yeast fermentation.

MENUS

SMORGASBORD

When you want to entertain with an especially grand buffet, a Swedish Smorgasbord is an impressive way to do it. Originating in Sweden at a time when each guest at a big country gathering brought food, it developed into an oppulent affair with dozens of dishes, especially in restaurants. For a home version in our country, a much simpler array is more practical; following, for example, the menu below. Whether the smorgasbord is simple or elaborate, the eating usually follows a certain order. First, guests serve themselves herring, a number of kinds being offered on the large buffets. With clean plates, guests then select a cold fish dish and a cucumber salad. Next is the cold meat course, with breads and other side dishes. Then the hot dishes are served, and finally a dessert. The typical beverage is beer, often with an akvavit toast at the beginning of the meal.

Cold Marinated Herring
Chilled Beer
Cold Salmon with Sour Cream Sauce
Cucumber Salad
Cold Cuts (sliced beef tongue, sausage, cheese)
Pickled Beets *Sliced Tomatoes*
Limpa Bread *Crisp Bread*
Swedish Meatballs
Boiled Potatoes with Fresh Dill
Scandinavian Fruit Soup
Coffee

Cold Salmon with Sour Cream Sauce

1 piece salmon (4 to 5 pounds)
3 quarts water
¼ cup lemon juice
3 tablespoons salt
1 cup dairy sour cream
2 teaspoons prepared horseradish
½ teaspoon sugar
½ teaspoon salt
Fresh parsley sprigs
Lemon wedges

1. Place salmon on a length of cheesecloth; tie ends securely.
2. Heat water, lemon juice, and 3 tablespoons salt to boiling in a fish poacher or large saucepot with a rack. Lower fish carefully into poacher so that it rests on the rack. Cover and simmer 10 to 15 minutes, or until fish flakes with a fork.
3. Carefully lift fish from poacher. Place in a shallow pan to cool. Chill in refrigerator.
4. For sauce, blend sour cream, horseradish, sugar, and ½ teaspoon salt. Chill thoroughly. (Increase sauce for larger piece of fish.)
5. To serve, remove fish carefully from cheesecloth. Place on serving platter. Scrape off skin, if any. Garnish with parsley and lemon wedges. Serve with sauce.

12 to 16 servings

Cucumber Salad

2 medium cucumbers
½ cup cider vinegar
⅓ cup water
⅓ cup sugar
½ teaspoon salt
　Dash white pepper
2 tablespoons minced fresh
　parsley

1. Score cucumbers by pulling tines of fork lengthwise down each cucumber. Cut into very thin slices; put into a bowl.
2. Mix vinegar, water, sugar, salt, and pepper. Pour over cucumbers. Chill several hours.
3. To serve, turn into a serving dish; sprinkle with parsley.

10 to 12 servings

Limpa Bread

2 packages active dry yeast
½ cup warm water (110° to 115°F)
½ cup packed brown sugar
⅓ cup molasses
1 tablespoon shortening
1 tablespoon salt
2 teaspoons caraway seed
½ teaspoon ground anise seed
1¼ cups hot water
5 to 5½ cups all-purpose flour
2 cups rye flour

1. Soften yeast in warm water.
2. In a large bowl, mix brown sugar, molasses, shortening, salt, and seeds. Stir in hot water. Let stand until lukewarm.
3. Add 1 cup flour; beat until smooth. Add yeast.
4. Add rye flour; beat until smooth. Stir in enough additional all-purpose flour to make a soft dough.
5. Turn out onto a lightly floured surface. Allow dough to rest 5 to 10 minutes. Knead until smooth and elastic. Form in a large ball. Place in a greased, deep bowl. Turn to bring greased surface to top. Cover and let stand in a warm place (85°F) until double in bulk.
6. Punch down. Turn onto floured surface. Shape into 2 oval loaves. Place on a greased cookie sheet. Cover and let rise until double in bulk.
7. Bake at 375°F 25 to 30 minutes, or until lightly browned. Cool.

2 loaves

Swedish Meatballs

2 pounds lean ground beef
1 pound ground lean pork
2 cups fine dry bread crumbs
1 cup mashed potatoes
2 eggs, slightly beaten
2 teaspoons salt
1 teaspoon brown sugar
½ teaspoon each allspice, nutmeg,
　and pepper
¼ teaspoon cloves
¼ teaspoon ginger
6 tablespoons butter or margarine
6 tablespoons flour
2 cups beef bouillon or stock
2 cups cream or milk

1. Lightly mix beef, pork, 1 cup crumbs, mashed potatoes, eggs, and seasonings.
2. Shape into balls about 1 inch in diameter. Roll in remaining 1 cup crumbs.
3. Brown meatballs in butter in a skillet, shaking frequently to brown evenly and to keep balls round. Remove from skillet.
4. Stir flour into fat in skillet. Stir in bouillon and cream. Cook, stirring constantly, until thickened. Season to taste, if needed.
5. Return meatballs to skillet. Cover and simmer about 15 minutes, or until meatballs are thoroughly cooked.

12 servings

Scandinavian Fruit Soup *(a dessert)*

2 cups dried apricots (11 ounces)
2 cups pitted dried prunes (11 ounces)
1 cup raisins (5 ounces)
1 quart water
2 cans or bottles (12 ounces each) beer
2 cups orange juice
½ cup sugar
2 cinnamon sticks
¼ cup cornstarch
Whipped cream and almonds (optional)

1. Place fruits, water, half of beer, orange juice, sugar, and cinnamon in a large saucepan. Heat to boiling; reduce heat, cover, and simmer 20 minutes.
2. Stir remaining beer into cornstarch; add to soup. Simmer 5 minutes more, stirring frequently, until fruit is tender and liquid is thickened and clear.
3. Serve cold. If desired, top with whipped cream and almonds.

10 cups

WINTER CHILI SUPPER

There's nothing quite as nice as a steaming bowl of spicy chili to warm one on a cold and wintry day. So when you ask friends to come for a casual chili supper, a cheery evening is certainly in store. Make an extra large quantity, for seconds will be in demand. Cold beer is a welcome complement to the hot chili, so you'll want to have plenty on hand. You also might like to begin the evening with a hot beer drink as a warmer when people first come in from the outdoors. To cool palates after the chili, a dessert of molded Spanish cream and fresh fruit would be fitting.

Hot Spiced Beer and Rum   *Cold Beer*

Cheddar Spritz Sticks
and/or Pickled Shrimp (page 34)

Chili con Cerveza

Crusty White Bread or Rolls (Mexican, French, Italian)

Tossed Green Salad

Molded Spanish Cream with Fresh Fruit

Coffee

Hot Spiced Beer and Rum

4 cans or bottles (12 ounces each) beer
1 cinnamon stick
8 whole cloves
Peel of ½ lemon, cut in strips
4 eggs
⅔ cup packed brown sugar
½ cup rum

1. Heat beer with cinnamon, cloves, and lemon peel for 10 to 15 minutes; do not simmer or boil.
2. Beat eggs with sugar until very thick.
3. Gradually add eggs to beer, stirring constantly. Stir in rum. Heat, but do not simmer or boil, stirring.
4. Serve immediately in small punch cups.

About 2 quarts

Shades o' Green Salad

8 ounces fresh spinach
½ head iceberg lettuce
4 celery stalks, sliced
1 green pepper, slivered
1 cucumber, sliced
2 tablespoons chopped chives
½ cup clear French dressing
8 pitted green olives, sliced
2 avocados, peeled and sliced

1. Line 8 to 10 individual salad bowls with spinach leaves. Tear remaining spinach and lettuce into pieces.
2. Toss lightly in a bowl the spinach, lettuce, celery, green pepper, cucumber, and chives. Pour dressing over salad; toss to coat evenly.
3. Arrange individual portions of salad in bowls; garnish each with olive and avocado slices.

8 to 10 servings

Irish Soda Bread with Currants

4 cups sifted all-purpose flour
2 tablespoons sugar
2 teaspoons baking soda
1½ teaspoons salt
¼ cup butter or margarine
⅔ cup dried currants, plumped
½ cup white vinegar
1 cup milk

1. Sift flour with sugar, baking soda, and salt. Cut in butter until crumbly. Stir in currants.
2. Mix vinegar and milk. Add half of liquid to dry ingredients, blend quickly. Add remaining liquid; stir only until blended.
3. Turn dough onto a floured surface. Lightly knead about 10 times. Shape into a round loaf. Place on a greased cookie sheet.
4. Bake at 375°F 35 to 40 minutes.

1 large loaf

FOURTH OF JULY PICNIC

The Fourth of July is a holiday when almost everyone feels like celebrating with a picnic. This menu is sure to be a success, for it is a collection of American picnic favorites, but with a few unusual touches. Beer subtly flavors the baked beans and the chili sauce, and a colorful fruit tart of red strawberries, white grapes, and blueberries becomes an eye-catching dessert. If you are going somewhere without cooking facilities, you could offer cold cuts and rye bread instead of hamburgers. Cold beer for adults and lemonade for the children are welcome thirst-quenchers.

Ice Cold Beer
Grilled Hamburgers in Buns with Beer Chili Sauce
(or Cold Cuts on Rye Bread)
Beans 'n' Beer Bake
Cole Slaw
Corn on the Cob (optional)
July 4th Fruit Tart

Beer Chili Sauce

½ cup beer
½ cup chili sauce
1 teaspoon Worcestershire sauce
1 teaspoon sugar
Dash Tabasco

1. Combine ingredients in a saucepan. Simmer, uncovered, 5 minutes.
2. Serve over hamburgers, frankfurters, bratwurst, or other link sausages in buns.

About ¾ cup

Beans 'n' Beer Bake

This "made from scratch" bean dish lazily bakes for hours in the oven to allow the flavors to blend and mellow.

1 pound dried navy beans
1 can or bottle (12 ounces) beer
½ pound salt pork or bacon, cut in 2-inch pieces
1 medium onion, quartered
2 tablespoons brown sugar
2 tablespoons molasses
2 tablespoons ketchup
2 teaspoons prepared mustard
1 teaspoon salt

1. Cover beans with water; soak overnight.
2. Drain beans; turn into a Dutch oven or large bean pot.
3. Combine remaining ingredients; stir into beans. Add water to cover beans.
4. Cover and bake at 275°F 5 to 6 hours, or until tender. Add water, if needed, during baking to keep beans covered with liquid. Remove cover during last 30 minutes; do not add additional water.

8 to 10 servings

July 4th Fruit Tart

Pastry for 2-crust pie
⅓ cup sugar
1 tablespoon cornstarch
⅔ cup water
1 tablespoon lemon juice
1 teaspoon butter or margarine
1 pint fresh strawberries, halved
1 pint fresh blueberries
1 cup halved white grapes

1. Roll pastry into a rectangle 4 inches longer and wider than overall size of an 11x7x1½-inch baking pan (or 4 inches longer and wider than a 9-inch square pan). Turn under extra pastry around top of pan; flute edge. Prick thoroughly with a fork.
2. Bake at 450°F 10 to 15 minutes.
3. For glaze, combine sugar and cornstarch in a saucepan. Stir in water and lemon juice. Cook, stirring constantly, until thickened and clear. Stir in butter. Cool to room temperature.
4. Spoon ¼ cup glaze over cooled pastry. Arrange alternate "stripes" of strawberries, blueberries, and grapes across narrow direction of pastry. Spoon remaining glaze over fruit. Chill.
5. To serve, cut so each person is served some of each fruit.

8 servings

BACKYARD BEER BASH

In the summertime entertaining turns supercasual with picnics, barbecues, patio suppers, block parties, community fairs, and so on. Whether you have an occasion to celebrate or not, it's a great time to invite a big group of friends to drop by, casually dressed, for a backyard beer bash. Offer a menu of bratwurst in beer, easy-to-serve accompaniments, and cold draught beer from a keg. The number of kegs you provide, will, of course, depend on the size of your crowd; see page 12.

Backyard Bratwurst in Beer for a Crowd

Buns   Spicy Mustard   Sauerkraut (optional)

Cold Potato Salad with Tart Dressing

Crisp Relishes

Watermelon

Draught Beer from a Keg

Backyard Bratwurst in Beer for a Crowd

2 **dozen unsmoked bratwurst**
2 **to 3 cans beer**
1 **tablespoon Worcestershire sauce**
2 **dozen frankfurter-style buns**
Spicy mustard

1. In a large pot, place bratwurst, enough beer to just cover, and Worcestershire sauce. Heat to boiling. Reduce heat, cover, and simmer 15 minutes.
2. Let bratwurst stand in beer about 1 hour.
3. Remove bratwurst from beer. Place on grill over hot coals. Grill just until browned. Serve in buns. Add mustard.

24 servings

Note: Sauerkraut may also be served alongside or in buns with bratwurst. Rinse and drain **5 pounds sauerkraut.** Simmer, uncovered, in some of the beer used for cooking the bratwurst, stirring occasionally, until most of the beer has evaporated. If desired, add 1 tablespoon caraway seed.

Cold Potato Salad with Tart Dressing

16 **medium potatoes (5 to 6 pounds)**
1 **dozen eggs, hard cooked**
2 **cups minced onion**
2 **cups diced cucumber**
1 **tablespoon salt**
1 **teaspoon pepper**

Dressing:
⅓ **cup flour**
1 **teaspoon sugar**
1 **teaspoon salt**
½ **teaspoon dry mustard**
Dash ground red pepper
1 **cup water**
¼ **cup vinegar or lemon juice**
1 **egg, slightly beaten**
1 **cup salad oil**

1. Wash potatoes. Place in a large kettle of boiling water to cover. Cover kettle and boil for 25˚ to 35 minutes, or until tender.
2. Peel potatoes while warm; cube. Cut hard-cooked eggs into eighths.
3. In a very large bowl, place cubed potatoes, eggs, onion, and cucumber. Sprinkle with salt and pepper.
4. For dressing, blend flour, sugar, and seasonings in a saucepan. Blend in water and vinegar. Cook, stirring constantly, to boiling; boil 2 minutes. Slowly pour cooked mixture into egg while beating. Continue beating while gradually adding oil.
5. Pour dressing over salad ingredients. Toss lightly; chill thoroughly.

24 servings

MEXICAN FIESTA PARTY

Beer is a very popular beverage in Mexico, probably because a glass of cerveza fria (cold beer) is such a nice foil for the hot and spicy foods. Thus when international party menus appropriate for serving with beer are being considered, Mexico certainly belongs on any list. A party with a Mexican theme is a gay and colorful event, too, and the foods lend themselves wonderfully to buffet service. Start with tantalizing spreads or dips for raw vegetables, tortilla chips, or crackers. Then proceed to the main course, with two entrées and several side dishes. Flan or baked caramel custard is a very traditional dessert in Mexico and Spain. The recipe yields are calculated for moderate-sized servings, since a variety of dishes to choose from appears on the table.

Cerveza Fria (Cold Beer)

Guacamole   Shrimp Spread (page 35)

Raw Vegetables   Tortilla Chips   Crackers

Pork and Beans, Mexican Style

Spiced Fruited Chicken

Baked Green Rice

Squash and Corn, Mexican Style

Soft Tortillas   Bolillos (Mexican Rolls)

Coconut Flan   Coffee

Pork and Beans, Mexican Style

½ pound sliced bacon
½ pound boneless lean pork, cubed
½ pound ham, cubed
2 large onions, sliced
3 cups peeled fresh or diced canned tomatoes
2 teaspoons chili powder (or more)
1 teaspoon cumin (comino)
1 teaspoon oregano
4 cups cooked or canned pinto or kidney beans, drained
2 cans or bottles (12 ounces each) beer

1. Cook bacon until crisp; drain and crumble.
2. In bacon fat, brown pork and ham. Add onion. Cover and cook until soft (about 5 minutes).
3. Add tomatoes, chili powder, cumin, oregano, and crumbled bacon. Add cooked beans; bring to boiling. Add beer gradually while stirring. Simmer uncovered about 1 hour, or until mixture is consistency of thick stew; stir occasionally.
4. Serve as a stew or on hot soft tortillas.

12 servings

Spiced Fruited Chicken

12 pieces frying chicken (breasts, legs, and thighs)
1½ teaspoons salt
¼ teaspoon each pepper, cinnamon, and cloves
2 garlic cloves, minced
¼ cup oil
½ cup chopped onion
1 can (13¼ ounces) crushed pineapple
1⅓ cups orange juice (about)
½ cup raisins
½ cup dry sherry

1. Rub chicken with mixture of salt, pepper, cinnamon, cloves, and garlic. Brown in oil in a heavy skillet.
2. Place browned chicken pieces in an attractive range-to-table Dutch oven.
3. Lightly brown onion in oil remaining in skillet.
4. Drain pineapple, reserving liquid. Add enough orange juice to liquid to measure 2 cups.
5. Add onion, pineapple, raisins, and orange juice mixture to chicken. Cover and simmer about 45 minutes, or until chicken is tender.
6. Remove chicken. Add sherry; cook uncovered 15 minutes longer to cook down liquid. Return chicken; heat through.

12 servings

Baked Green Rice

3 cups hot cooked rice
2 cups (8 ounces) shredded Monterey Jack or mild Cheddar cheese
⅓ cup butter or margarine
1 can (4 ounces) green chilies, drained, seeded, and chopped
1 cup finely chopped parsley
1 large onion, chopped
1 teaspoon salt
¼ teaspoon pepper
2 eggs, beaten
1 cup milk

1. Combine hot rice with cheese and butter. Toss until well mixed. Add chilies, parsley, onion, salt, and pepper; mix.
2. Mix eggs and milk; stir into rice mixture. Turn into a buttered 2-quart baking dish.
3. Cover and bake at 350°F 30 minutes. Uncover; bake 10 minutes more.

12 servings

Squash and Corn, Mexican Style

½ cup chopped onion
1 garlic clove, minced
2 tablespoons oil
2 pounds yellow summer squash, cubed
1 can (16 ounces) whole kernel corn, drained
2 medium fresh tomatoes, peeled and cubed
1 jalapeño chili, finely chopped
1 teaspoon salt
¼ teaspoon pepper
½ cup milk
Grated Parmesan cheese

1. In a skillet that can be transferred to oven, cook onion and garlic in oil until soft (about 5 minutes).
2. Add squash, corn, tomatoes, chili, salt, and pepper. Cook over low heat, stirring occasionally, about 10 minutes. Pour milk over top. (If skillet cannot be put in oven, transfer to baking dish.)
3. Bake at 350°F about 30 minutes. Sprinkle with Parmesan cheese.

12 servings

Coconut Flan

Caramel Topping:
    1 cup granulated sugar
    ¼ cup water

Custard:
    4 cups milk
    8 eggs
    ½ cup sugar
    ¼ teaspoon salt
    1 teaspoon vanilla extract
    ⅔ cup shredded or flaked coconut

1. If you have only 6 custard cups, prepare ½ recipe at a time.
2. For caramel topping, heat sugar and water in a heavy skillet, stirring constantly, until sugar melts and turns golden brown.
3. Pour syrup into 12 custard cups or two 1-quart casseroles. Tip cups or casseroles to coat bottom and part way up sides.
4. For custard, scald milk. Beat eggs; beat in sugar, salt, and vanilla extract. Gradually beat scalded milk into egg mixture. Strain into prepared cups or casseroles. Sprinkle with coconut.
5. Place in a pan containing hot water which comes at least 1 inch up sides of cups or casseroles.
6. Bake at 325°F 45 minutes for cups, or 1 hour for casseroles.
7. Cool. Invert on serving platter. Chill.

12 servings

TAILGATE FOOTBALL PICNIC

Tailgate picnics in the parking lot before fall football games have become quite a popular part of the pregame festivities and excitement. The food should be fairly simple, yet with a few out-of-ordinary touches to make the event memorable. The menu suggested here should do just that, for it puts together several convenience foods in an intriguing manner. Beer tastily flavors a canned cheese soup. Beer again goes into the gingerbread mix which becomes a pear upside-down cake—although not much beer flavor comes through. Naturally, the pregame beverage is cold beer. To share the work load, the various couples participating might each bring one of the foods.

Easy Beer-Cheese Soup (from a thermos)

**Sliced Ham and Sausage
on Kaiser Rolls**

Marinated Bean Salad

Gingerbread Pear Upside-down Cake

Cold Beer

Easy Beer-Cheese Soup

2 cans (10½ ounces each)
  condensed cream soup, such
  as celery, mushroom, or
  chicken
1 teaspoon Worcestershire sauce
¼ teaspoon seasoned salt
¼ teaspoon paprika
2 cans or bottles (12 ounces each)
  beer
2 cups shredded Cheddar cheese
  (8 ounces)
  Garnish (optional)

1. In a saucepan, mix soup and seasonings. Add beer gradually while stirring. Heat to simmering.
2. Add cheese. Heat slowly, stirring constantly, until cheese is melted.
3. Pour into soup bowls or cups. Garnish as desired with **croutons, bacon bits, minced parsley,** or **chives.**

7 cups; about 8 servings

Marinated Bean Salad

½ cup cider vinegar
⅓ cup sugar
1 teaspoon salt
1 can (16 ounces) cut green
  beans, drained
1 can (16 ounces) cut wax beans,
  drained
1 can (16 ounces) kidney beans,
  rinsed and drained
1 medium onion, quartered and
  finely sliced
1 medium green pepper, chopped
  (optional)
⅓ cup salad oil
¼ teaspoon pepper

1. Blend vinegar, sugar, and salt in a small saucepan. Heat until sugar is dissolved.
2. Place all beans, onion, green pepper, vinegar mixture, oil, and pepper in a large nonmetal container. Toss to coat evenly.
3. Chill several hours or overnight, stirring occasionally.

8 to 12 servings

Gingerbread Pear Upside-down Cake

The use of a package mix makes this a very simple cake.

2 tablespoons butter or margarine
⅓ cup packed brown sugar
2 medium pears, pared and sliced
1 package (14 to 14½ ounces)
  gingerbread mix
1 to 1¼ cups beer
1 egg (if specified for mix)

1. Melt butter in an 8-inch square pan. Stir in brown sugar; spread evenly over bottom of pan. Arrange pear slices in rows over sugar.
2. Mix gingerbread according to package directions, substituting an equal amount of beer for the amount of water specified and adding egg if called for.
3. Pour batter over pears.
4. Bake at 350°F 40 to 45 minutes, or until cake tests done. Immediately loosen cake from sides of pan and invert on a serving platter. Serve warm.

8 servings

OKTOBERFEST DINNER PARTY

Oktoberfest has been celebrated in Munich, Germany, since the early 1800's as a massive fall festival of beer drinking, eating, and amusement park delights. Originally a celebration observing the marriage of Crown Prince Ludwig of Bavaria, it now lasts more than two weeks in late September and early October.

If you are planning a dinner party in the fall, Oktoberfest would be an appropriate and fun theme to follow. Your guests are bound to have a good time and go away cheered by the delicious, hearty German food. Cold beer is, of course, the only suitable beverage. This menu is designed for a medium-sized group and could be increased somewhat. But for a large crowd or a more casual evening to celebrate Oktoberfest, refer to the Backyard Beer Bash menu and add a bakery cheese cake for dessert.

Beer in Steins

Hot German Beer Soup or Cups of Lentil Soup

German Pork Roast in Spicy Beer Sauce

Caraway Dumplings or Buttered Noodles

Sweet-Sour Red Cabbage

Dark Rye Bread

Cucumber Salad with Sour Cream

Hazelnut Torte with Creamy Rum Filling   *Coffee*

Hot German Beer Soup (Heisse Biersuppe)

  3 cans or bottles (12 ounces each) beer
  2 to 4 tablespoons sugar
  2 egg yolks
  1 cup dairy sour cream
  ¼ cup flour
  ½ teaspoon cinnamon
  ¼ teaspoon salt
  Dash pepper
  4 large slices rye bread
  ½ cup shredded Muenster or brick cheese

1. In a large, heavy saucepan, heat beer and sugar until sugar dissolves.
2. Beat egg yolks, sour cream, flour, cinnamon, salt, and pepper until smooth. Add a little hot beer mixture; blend.
3. Gradually stir into hot beer. Cook slowly, stirring constantly, until thickened.
4. With bottom of beer can or a biscuit cutter, cut rounds out of rye bread; sprinkle with cheese. Broil just until melted.
5. Pour soup into small bowls; top with cheesy rye rounds.

8 servings

German Pork Roast in Spicy Beer Sauce

1 rolled pork loin roast, boneless
    (3 to 3½ pounds)
2 to 3 cups beer
1 cup chopped onion
2 teaspoons grated lemon peel
2 teaspoons sugar
1 teaspoon tarragon
1 teaspoon salt
¼ teaspoon each pepper, cloves,
    ginger, and nutmeg
3 bay leaves
1 carrot, diced
1 celery stalk, diced
¼ cup flour

1. Place meat in a deep dish just large enough to hold it. Combine 1 can (1½ cups) beer, onion, peel, and seasonings; pour over meat. Add a little more beer, if needed, to just cover meat. Marinate in refrigerator 1 to 2 days, turning occasionally.
2. Strain marinade, reserving solids and liquid. Place solids, carrot, and celery in bottom of a roasting pan. Place meat on top. Add a little liquid.
3. Roast in a 350°F oven 1 hour. Pour one quarter of remaining marinade liquid over meat. Continue roasting for 1 to 1½ hours more, basting occasionally with drippings and more marinade, until meat thermometer registers 170°F.
4. Mix flour and ⅓ cup marinade or beer to a smooth paste. Place roast on a platter; keep warm. Skim fat from cooking liquid. Strain, pressing solids; add flour mixture and ½ cup beer plus water, if needed, to measure 2 cups total liquid. Cook in roasting pan or a saucepan, stirring constantly, until thickened. (For 3 cups gravy, use more beer and water plus 6 tablespoons flour.) Serve sauce over meat slices.

8 servings

Caraway Dumplings

1 quart water
2 chicken bouillon cubes
2 cups all-purpose flour
2 tablespoons dried parsley flakes
4 teaspoons baking powder
2 teaspoons caraway seed
½ teaspoon salt
3 tablespoons butter or margarine
1 cup milk or beer

1. In a wide, large pot, heat water and bouillon cubes to boiling, stirring to dissolve.
2. Mix dry ingredients; cut in butter until crumbly. Stir in milk or beer. If using beer, remainder of can may be added to bouillon.
3. Drop 8 large spoonfuls onto boiling bouillon. Reduce heat to medium. Cover and steam 15 minutes; do not peek.

8 servings

Note: Caraway Dumplings may also be made to top hearty, main-dish soups. Divide recipe in half, and drop 4 to 6 spoonfuls onto boiling soup. Cover and steam 15 minutes, reducing heat to medium; do not peek.

Sweet-Sour Red Cabbage

1 head red cabbage (about 2
    pounds)
1½ cups water
⅓ cup packed brown sugar
1 teaspoon salt
    Dash pepper
¼ cup vinegar
¼ cup butter or margarine

1. Discard wilted outer leaves of cabbage. Cut into quarters, discarding core. Coarsely shred.
2. Place cabbage in a saucepan with water, brown sugar, salt, and pepper. Cover loosely and simmer 20 to 30 minutes, or until cabbage is tender and most of liquid has evaporated. Boil down without lid a few minutes, if necessary.
3. Add vinegar and butter; toss until butter is melted.

8 to 10 servings

Cucumber Salad with Sour Cream

2 large cucumbers
1 cup dairy sour cream
3 tablespoons vinegar
2 tablespoons minced chives
1 teaspoon salt
¼ teaspoon white pepper

1. Score cucumbers ⅛ inch deep with fork. Slice.
2. Mix remaining ingredients. Toss with cucumber slices. Chill. If desired, garnish salad with sieved hard-cooked egg yolk.   *8 to 10 servings*

Hazelnut Torte

½ pound hazelnuts or filberts (1½ cups), grated or ground
½ cup all-purpose flour
½ teaspoon instant coffee
½ teaspoon unsweetened cocoa
6 eggs, separated
¼ teaspoon salt
1 cup sugar
1 teaspoon grated lemon peel
1 teaspoon rum or brandy
½ teaspoon vanilla extract
Creamy Rum Filling

1. Reserve ¼ cup ground nuts for topping. Combine remaining nuts, flour, instant coffee, and cocoa. Turn onto waxed paper; with a spatula mark into 4 portions.
2. Beat egg whites and salt until foamy. Gradually add ½ cup sugar, continuing beating until stiff peaks form.
3. In a separate bowl, combine egg yolks, ½ cup sugar, peel, rum, and vanilla extract. (Beater does not have to be washed from beating white.) Beat until very thick and lemon colored.
4. Gently spread yolk mixture over beaten whites. Spoon one portion of flour-nut mixture over eggs; gently fold until only partially blended. Repeat with remaining three portions, folding just until blended after last addition. Do not overmix.
5. Gently turn into 2 greased and waxed-paper-lined 9-inch round layer cake pans.
6. Bake at 350°F 25 to 30 minutes, or until torte tests done. Cool in pans. Remove.
7. Prepare Creamy Rum Filling; chill. Place one torte layer on serving plate; spread with half of filling. Add second layer; top with second half of filling. Sprinkle with reserved nuts.

One 9-inch torte

Creamy Rum Filling

⅓ cup sugar
2½ tablespoons flour
¼ teaspoon salt
1½ cups cream or half-and-half
3 egg yolks, slightly beaten
2 tablespoons rum
1 tablespoon butter

1. In top of a double boiler, combine sugar, flour, and salt. Stir in cream. Cook, stirring constantly, to boiling. Boil and stir 2 minutes.
2. Place over simmering water. Cover and cook 5 to 7 minutes, stirring occasionally.
3. Add a little hot mixture to egg yolks. Stir into mixture in double boiler. Cook over simmering water, stirring constantly, 3 to 5 minutes.
4. Stir in rum and butter. Cover surface with waxed paper. Cool, then chill thoroughly.

About 1⅔ cups filling

HOLIDAY OPEN HOUSE

A bowl of steaming hot wassail is an old English Christmas tradition dating back centuries; it's even celebrated in verse and song. There are a number of versions of wassail, but one of the ingredients in an authentic wassail is English ale or beer. Often apples float on top.

In the United States wassail is not very common, thus providing you with an idea for a holiday open-house beverage that is appropriate, yet will set your party apart from the many others of the season. You will probably also want a buffet spread of festive nibbling foods. Two tasty sweets are beer-flavored fruitcake and Beer Balls, which are similar to rum or bourbon balls. The balance of your spread could include assorted cheeses, favorite appetizers (from the appetizer chapter in this book, if you choose), and other favorite Christmas cookies and confections.

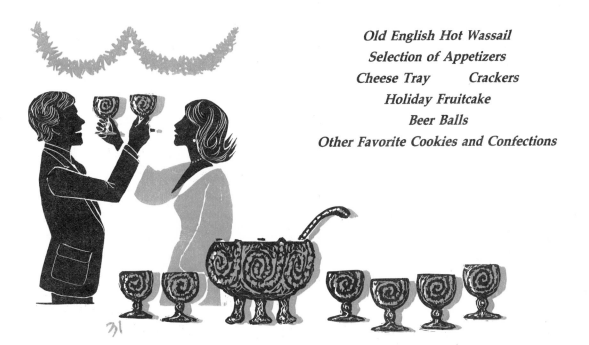

Old English Hot Wassail
Selection of Appetizers
Cheese Tray   Crackers
Holiday Fruitcake
Beer Balls
Other Favorite Cookies and Confections

Old English Hot Wassail

Increase the recipe as needed for the size of your crowd, but don't pour too much at one time into the punch bowl; servings should be piping hot.

6 bottles (12 ounces each) ale
1½ to 2 cups sugar
  Thin strips peel from 1 lemon
6 whole cloves
6 whole allspice
1 cinnamon stick
1 whole nutmeg, cracked
  (optional)
1 bottle (25.4 ounces) dry sherry
  Small baked apples or lemon
  slices

1. Place 2 bottles ale, sugar, lemon peel, and spices in a kettle. Heat below simmering for at least 30 minutes. (Wassail is even better if this mixture can stand for several hours before proceeding.)

2. Add sherry and remaining ale. Heat, but do not simmer or boil.

3. Pour into a punch bowl. Float small baked apples or lemon slices in punch. Serve in punch cups.

3 quarts; 24 half-cup servings

Holiday Fruitcake

1½ cups sifted all-purpose flour
1 teaspoon baking powder
1 teaspoon cinnamon
½ teaspoon ginger
½ teaspoon nutmeg
⅛ teaspoon salt
1 cup chopped mixed candied fruit (6 ounces)
1 cup raisins (5 ounces)
¾ cup chopped walnuts
½ cup butter or margarine
¾ cup packed brown sugar
1 egg
½ cup beer
Halved candied cherries (optional)

1. Sift together dry ingredients. Mix a little with fruits and nuts.
2. Cream butter and brown sugar. Add egg; beat well.
3. Add remaining dry ingredients alternately with beer; beat until smooth.
4. Add fruits and nuts; stir by hand.
5. Turn into greased and waxed-paper-lined pans: three 5½x3x2-inch fruitcake pans, or one 9x5x3-inch loaf pan. Decorate tops with candied cherries, if desired.
6. Bake at 275°F 1¼ hours for small pans, or 1¾ to 2 hours for a 9x5-inch pan, or until done. Cool 20 minutes in pans. Turn out on wire racks.
7. Wrap each fruitcake in cheesecloth soaked in additional beer, then wrap in foil. Age in refrigerator at least 2 weeks, basting occasionally with beer.

3 small or 1 large

Beer Balls

Instead of brandy or rum balls, why not try these tasty beer balls for a holiday-season treat? They are better after a day or so in the refrigerator.

1 box (7¼ ounces) vanilla wafers (about 55), finely crushed
1 cup ground walnuts (3 ounces)
1 cup confectioners' sugar
⅓ cup beer
2 tablespoons corn syrup or honey
Confectioners' sugar for coating

1. Mix wafer crumbs, nuts, and 1 cup confectioners' sugar.
2. Mix beer and corn syrup, add to wafer mixture, and stir.
3. Shape into 1-inch balls. Chill at least 1 day. Roll in additional confectioners' sugar.

About 3½ dozen

APPETIZERS

Whether preceding a dinner or served as nibbling foods at a cocktail party, appetizers and hors d'oeuvres made with beer lend a festive touch. Beer and cheese are perfect partners, so several beer-flavored cheese recipes are included. Seafood, sausages, and mushrooms are other suggestions. Cheddar Spritz Sticks, Shamrock Canapés, and Swedish Meatballs are appetizer ideas that appear in the menu section of this book. In the cheese chapter are Dutch Fondue and a Welsh Rabbit that could be used as a dip. The fritter batter in the bread chapter could be used on vegetables, meat cubes, or shrimp for hors d'oeuvres.

Beer can be the chosen beverage. Or these appetizers go nicely with other drinks. You might want to serve the beer in some manner other than straight from the can, bottle, or keg. If so, turn to the beverages chapter for some unusual ideas.

Appetizer Puffs

These tiny cream puffs may be filled as you wish to make dainty and appealing hors d'oeuvres.

1 cup beer
½ cup butter or margarine
½ teaspoon salt
1 cup all-purpose flour
4 eggs

1. Heat beer, butter, and salt to boiling in a saucepan.
2. Add flour all at once. Beat vigorously with a wooden spoon until mixture leaves sides of pan and forms a smooth ball.
3. Add eggs, one at a time, beating until smooth.
4. Drop mixture by rounded teaspoonfuls onto a greased cookie sheet, 1 inch apart.
5. Bake at 450°F 10 minutes. Turn oven control to 350°F and bake 5 to 10 minutes more, or until lightly browned and puffed.
6. Cool. Split and fill with desired filling: Shrimp Spread (page 35), ham salad, crab or tuna salad, German Beer Cheese (page 36), etc.

About 40 puffs

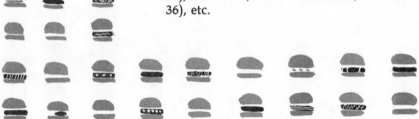

Pickled Shrimp

With small to medium shrimp, serve this appetizer on cocktail rye rounds. Larger shrimp may be served on fancy picks.

1 can or bottle (12 ounces) beer
¼ cup oil
1 tablespoon lemon juice
1 teaspoon sugar
1 teaspoon salt
½ teaspoon each dill seed, dry mustard, and celery salt
¼ teaspoon tarragon
⅛ teaspoon ground red pepper
2 bay leaves, halved
2 medium onions, chopped
1 package (10 ounces) small to medium frozen cooked shrimp, thawed

1. Place all ingredients except shrimp in a saucepan. Simmer 10 to 15 minutes, or until onions are just tender.
2. Add shrimp; remove from heat. Turn into a small casserole. Cover and refrigerate at least 1 day.
3. Remove bay leaves; drain off marinade. Let guests spoon shrimp and onions onto **cocktail rye rounds.**

About 25 appetizers

Note: With larger shrimp to be served on fancy picks, use only one onion and slice it. Remove onion before serving. Recipe may also be made with uncooked shrimp. Add them 4 to 5 minutes before end of cooking time; cover and simmer until shrimp turn pink. Continue as in above recipe.

Shrimp Dunk

This is the famous shrimp boiled in beer served as an appetizer. Instead of cocktail sauce or melted butter, try cold beer for dunking.

1 can or bottle (12 ounces) beer
    plus ½
    cup water
1 small onion, sliced
    Top and leaves of 1 stalk celery
1 tablespoon salt
3 or 4 peppercorns
1 bay leaf
1 garlic clove
1 pound very large shelled
    shrimp, uncooked

1. Combine ingredients except shrimp in a large saucepan. Cover; heat to boiling. Boil 10 minutes.
2. Add shrimp. Cover and boil 5 minutes, or just until shrimp turn pink. Remove from heat; chill in cooking liquid.
3. Serve cold with dunking bowls of cold beer. Serve as hors d'oeuvres or as a summertime main entrée.

25 to 30 shrimp

Shrimp Spread

Serve this spread at a cocktail party—on fancy crackers or inside tiny beer-flavored cream puffs.

½ cup butter or margarine,
    softened
2 green onions with some tops
2 parsley sprigs
¼ teaspoon salt
⅛ teaspoon garlic powder
    Dash pepper
1 package (12 ounces) frozen
    cooked shrimp, thawed
½ cup beer
1 tablespoon capers (optional)
    Fancy crackers or tiny cream
    puffs

1. Using a food processor or blender, process butter, onions, parsley, and seasonings until vegetables are minced and mixture is smooth. (With blender, prepare in 2 or 3 batches.)
2. Add shrimp, beer, and capers. Process to a smooth paste.
3. Serve at room temperature on crackers or in tiny cream puffs. Use a rounded teaspoon for each. (One half recipe of Shrimp Spread fills one recipe Appetizer Puffs (page 34).

2¾ cups spread for about 7 dozen crackers or tiny cream puffs

Marinated Mushrooms

Serve hot or cold as light hors d'oeuvres before a dinner party, or as part of an array of cocktail party nibbling foods.

1 pound small fresh mushrooms
⅔ cup vegetable oil
½ cup beer
¼ cup minced green onion with
    tops
2 tablespoons lemon juice
1 tablespoon chopped parsley
1 large garlic clove, minced
½ teaspoon salt
    Dash pepper

1. Wash mushrooms, remove stems, and pat dry. Reserve stems for later use.
2. Combine remaining ingredients in a shallow glass or ceramic dish. Add mushrooms. Cover and let stand at room temperature about 3 hours, stirring occasionally.
3. Place mushrooms, cup side up, on a broiler pan. Spoon some marinade over each. Broil 3 inches from heat about 2 minutes, or until lightly browned. Serve warm with picks.

40 to 50 mushrooms

Note: Marinated Mushrooms may also be served cold. Marinate in refrigerator. Do not broil. Turn into a serving bowl with marinade; serve with picks. Canned button mushrooms may also be used when serving this dish cold.

Tangy Cheese Dip

4 ounces Muenster cheese or other semisoft cheese, finely shredded (1 cup)
3 ounces blue cheese, crumbled
1 package (3 ounces) cream cheese, softened
⅛ teaspoon garlic powder
¾ cup beer (about)

1. After shredding, let Muenster cheese stand at room temperature at least 1 hour.
2. Using an electric blender or food processor, blend cheeses and garlic. Gradually add enough beer to make a mixture of dipping consistency.
3. Serve at room temperature with crackers for dipping.

About 2 cups

German Beer Cheese (Bierkäse)

Serve as a spread for hors d'oeuvres at a party or before dinner. It's especially good on rye rounds with glasses of cold beer to drink.

½ pound Cheddar cheese
½ pound Swiss cheese
2 teaspoons Worcestershire sauce
1 teaspoon dry mustard
1 small garlic clove, mashed
½ cup beer (about)

1. Shred cheeses finely. Or put through a meat grinder, using finest blade.
2. Add Worcestershire sauce, dry mustard, garlic, and enough beer to make a mixture of spreading consistency.
3. Turn into a 3-cup rounded bowl or mold; pack firmly. Chill. Unmold and serve at room temperature with **small rye rounds** or **crackers.**

3 cups

Cocktail Party Sausages

1½ cups Mustard Sauce or Savory Barbecue Sauce (pages 73, 72)
4 dozen (about) cocktail frankfurters, vienna sausages, cocktail smoked sausage links, or chunks of frankfurters

1. Prepare desired sauce and heat with your choice of sausage.
2. Turn into a chafing dish. Serve warm with decorative picks.

About 4 dozen

Chili Nuts

These zippy nuts are nice to nibble on while drinking a glass of cold beer.

1 package (12 ounces) shelled raw peanuts
2 tablespoons peanut or vegetable oil
2 teaspoons chili powder
1 teaspoon salt

1. Combine ingredients in a large baking pan; spread thinly.
2. Bake at 325°F 25 minutes. Cool on waxed paper.

2 cups

BREADS

Marvelously delectable things happen when beer is used as the liquid in baking breads of various kinds. In some, a hint of the zesty beer flavor remains after baking. In others, the beer flavor is almost undetectable, but the texture is delightful. Compared to baked products using milk as the liquid, breads baked with beer seem to possess a more tender crumb and a lighter texture. The same is true of cakes (see Desserts).

This chapter offers tantalizing recipes for a whole gamut of beer breads: yeast breads, quick breads, biscuits, muffins, cornbread, pancakes, waffles, and fritters. After you have tried some of them, you might enjoy experimenting on your own by substituting beer for the liquid in other bread recipes. Some nice surprises will be in store. Two bread recipes using beer, Cheddar Spritz Sticks and Caraway Dumplings, appear in the menu section.

Streusel Coffeecake

Coffeecake:
    2 cups all-purpose biscuit mix
    ½ cup sugar
    ⅔ cup beer
    1 egg, slightly beaten
Topping:
    ½ cup flour
    ⅓ cup sugar
    1 teaspoon cinnamon
    ⅓ cup butter or margarine

1. For coffeecake, combine biscuit mix and sugar. Mix beer and egg.
2. Add beer mixture to dry mixture. Stir lightly, just until moistened. Turn into a greased 9-inch round cake pan.
3. For streusel topping, combine flour, sugar, and cinnamon. Cut in butter until crumbly. Sprinkle over coffeecake batter.
4. Bake at 400°F 25 minutes. Serve warm or cooled.

1 coffeecake

Beer-Cheese Bread with Raisins

A sweet, moist quick bread to serve for breakfast or with afternoon tea.

    1 cup raisins (5 ounces)
    1 can or bottle (12 ounces) beer
2½ cups all-purpose flour
    ¾ cup sugar
    1 tablespoon baking powder
    ½ teaspoon baking soda
    ½ teaspoon salt
    4 ounces Cheddar cheese, finely
        shredded
    ¼ cup oil
    1 egg

1. Heat raisins and beer to simmering. Remove from heat; let stand about 10 minutes.
2. Combine dry ingredients. Add cheese; stir to coat.
3. Mix oil and egg. Add to dry ingredients, along with beer and raisins. Beat just until blended.
4. Turn into a greased and floured 9x5x3-inch loaf pan.
5. Bake at 350°F 1 hour. Turn out on a rack to cool. Cool thoroughly before slicing.

1 loaf

Jiffy Beer Bread

Only three ingredients and a few seconds of mixing create a quick bread ready for the oven. Serve it warm with butter and jam, if you wish.

    3 cups self-rising flour
    3 tablespoons sugar
    1 can or bottle (12 ounces) beer

1. Mix self-rising flour and sugar; make a well in center.
2. Add beer. Stir until just blended.
3. Turn into a greased 9x5x3-inch loaf pan.
4. Bake at 350°F 50 minutes, or until done. Turn out immediately. Cool on a rack.

1 loaf

Bock Beer Bread

Make this hearty bread in the springtime when bock beer is available. Or substitute dark beer or light beer plus ½ teaspoon molasses.

1 cup bock beer
1 package active dry yeast
3¼ cups all-purpose flour (about)
3 tablespoons butter or
    margarine, softened
3 tablespoons brown sugar
1 egg
1 teaspoon salt
½ cup toasted wheat germ

1. Warm the beer to about 110° to 115°F; pour into a large bowl. Sprinkle with yeast; let stand 5 minutes.
2. Add 1½ cups flour, butter, brown sugar, egg, and salt. Beat until smooth, using electric mixer if desired.
3. Stir in wheat germ and enough flour to make a soft dough. Turn out onto floured board. Knead 5 to 10 minutes until smooth and elastic.
4. Place dough in a greased bowl. Cover and let rise in a warm place until double in bulk (about 1 hour).
5. Punch down. Shape into a loaf; place in a greased 9x5x3-inch loaf pan. Cover and let rise until double in bulk (about 1 hour).
6. Bake at 325°F 30 minutes, or until done. Remove from pan; cool on a rack.

1 loaf

Peasant Black Bread

Beer is not the only surprise ingredient in these hearty loaves.

3¾ cups rye flour
3¾ cups all-purpose flour
2 packages active dry yeast
2 tablespoons caraway seed,
    crushed
½ teaspoon fennel seed, crushed
4 teaspoons onion salt (or 2
    teaspoons onion powder and
    2 teaspoons salt)
2 teaspoons instant coffee
2½ cups beer
¼ cup vinegar
¼ cup butter or margarine
¼ cup dark molasses
1 ounce (1 square) unsweetened
    chocolate

1. Combine flours. In a large bowl, mix half of flour mixture with yeast, caraway seed, fennel seed, onion salt, and coffee.
2. In a saucepan, combine beer, vinegar, butter, molasses, and chocolate. Heat slowly until mixture is very warm (120° to 130°F); butter and chocolate need not be melted.
3. Add warm ingredients to flour-yeast mixture. Beat with electric mixer about 2 minutes, using medium speed. Add ½ cup reserved flour mixture; beat on high speed about 2 minutes.
4. Add enough additional flour to make a stiff dough, stirring by hand when dough becomes thick.
5. Turn onto lightly floured surface; let rest 10 minutes. Knead about 10 minutes, or until smooth and elastic.
6. Form into a ball; place in a greased bowl, turning once to grease top. Cover and let rise in warm place (80° to 85°F) until double in bulk (about 1 hour).
7. Punch down; turn onto a lightly floured surface. Divide in half; shape each half into a ball about 5 inches in diameter. Place each in center of a greased 8-inch round cake pan. Or place on greased cookie sheets. Cover and let rise until double in bulk (about 1 hour).
8. Bake at 350°F about 45 minutes, or until done. Remove from pans; cool on racks.

2 loaves

Old-Style Cornbread

If you can find coarse, stone-ground cornmeal, it makes a marvelous cornbread. You can't taste the beer in this recipe, but it gives a moist and tender texture to the bread.

1 cup yellow cornmeal
   (preferably coarse
   stone-ground)
1 cup all-purpose flour
2 tablespoons sugar
1 tablespoon baking powder
½ teaspoon salt
1¼ cups beer
¼ cup bacon drippings
1 egg, slightly beaten
2 tablespoons diced cracklings or
   crisp-cooked bacon (optional)

1. Combine dry ingredients.
2. Add beer, drippings, egg, and cracklings. Stir lightly, just until moistened.
3. Turn into a greased 8-inch square baking pan.
4. Bake at 375°F 20 to 25 minutes, or until done.

9 servings

Beer Griddlecakes with Pilgrim Syrup

The syrup for these intriguing griddlecakes dates back to colonial times.

Batter:
1¾ cups all-purpose flour
1½ teaspoons baking powder
½ teaspoon baking soda
½ teaspoon salt
1 egg
3 tablespoons oil
1 tablespoon molasses
1 can or bottle (12 ounces) beer
Pilgrim Syrup:
1 cup packed brown sugar
½ cup beer
1 tablespoon butter (optional)

1. For batter, mix flour, baking powder, baking soda, and salt.
2. Beat egg with oil and molasses. Add to dry ingredients along with beer. Stir lightly, just until blended. Batter will be slightly lumpy and somewhat thick.
3. Using about 2 tablespoons batter for each griddlecake, spoon batter onto hot and very lightly greased griddle. Spread with back of spoon to 3½ to 4 inches in diameter. Cook until browned, turning once.
4. For syrup, combine ingredients in a saucepan. Boil about 2 minutes. Makes ⅔ cup syrup.

20 griddlecakes; 4 or 5 servings

Danish Pancakes

Traditionally a dessert, these delicious filled pancakes may also be served at brunch.

1 cup all-purpose biscuit mix
1 egg, slightly beaten
¾ cup beer
⅓ cup milk
   Jam, jelly, or preserves
   Sifted confectioners' sugar

1. Combine biscuit mix, egg, beer, and milk, stirring just until blended. Batter will be slightly lumpy.
2. Using about 1 tablespoon batter per pancake, cook on a very lightly greased griddle or skillet until lightly browned, turning once.
3. Spread with jam. Roll up. Sprinkle with confectioners' sugar. Serve warm.

20 small pancakes; 4 to 6 servings

Brussels Waffles *(Gaufres Bruxelloises)*

These waffles are a crisp type and are often served for dessert topped with sweetened whipped cream and strawberries. They became famous at the Belgian pavilion at the 1962 New York World's Fair.

1¾ cups all-purpose flour
⅛ teaspoon salt
1 can or bottle (12 ounces) beer
¼ cup oil
1 egg, slightly beaten
1 tablespoon grated lemon peel
½ teaspoon lemon juice
½ teaspoon vanilla extract

1. Mix flour and salt; add remaining ingredients. Beat just until smooth.
2. Let batter stand 2 hours at room temperature or refrigerate overnight. (Makes waffles more tender.) Waffles may also be baked immediately.
3. Bake in a waffle iron, following manufacturer's directions. Spread batter thin; bake until crisp and browned. Separate waffles into sections.
4. Serve for dessert or breakfast. Top with sweetened whipped cream and strawberries or brown sugar.

Note: Yield depends upon size of waffle iron. For example, with one that makes 7-inch rounds, recipe will make 4 large rounds that separate into 16 sections.

Beer-Can Biscuits

These flaky biscuits are flavored with a hint of beer and cut out with an opened beer can.

2 cups all-purpose flour
1 tablespoon baking powder
½ teaspoon salt
⅓ cup lard or shortening
¾ cup beer

1. Combine dry ingredients. Cut in lard until crumbly.
2. Add beer. Stir with a fork until dough follows fork and forms a ball.
3. Turn onto a floured board. Knead 10 to 12 times. Roll out ½ inch thick (no thinner). Cut out with beer can, opened on bottom; or use a 2½-inch biscuit cutter. Reroll scraps.
4. Place on an ungreased cookie sheet. Brush with beer.
5. Bake at 450°F 10 to 12 minutes, or until lightly browned.
12 biscuits

Note: Dough may be used as topping for a meat pie. Roll or pat out to fit casserole. Add during last 10 to 15 minutes of baking time.

Cheese-Beer Biscuits

These quick biscuits perked up with cheese, green onions, and beer will be a nice surprise for lunch or dinner. The dough is cut into squares; hence, no wasted dough or scraps to reroll.

2 cups all-purpose biscuit mix
½ cup shredded Cheddar cheese
¼ cup minced green onion with part of tops (3 or 4 onions)
⅔ cup beer

1. Combine biscuit mix, cheese, and green onion.
2. Add beer; stir with fork until dough forms a ball (it will be sticky). Turn out onto a well-floured board; knead 10 to 12 times.
3. Roll or pat into an even square ½ inch thick. Cut into 16 small squares. Place on lightly greased baking sheet.
4. Bake at 450°F 10 to 12 minutes, or until lightly browned. Serve warm.

16 biscuits

Orange Muffins

A slight tang of beer underlies the orange flavor in these tasty muffins. Serve them hot from the oven.

2 cups all-purpose flour
1 tablespoon baking powder
¼ teaspoon salt
⅛ teaspoon ginger
¾ cup beer
½ cup orange marmalade
¼ cup oil or melted shortening
1 egg, slightly beaten

1. Combine dry ingredients; make a well in center.
2. Combine beer, marmalade, oil, and egg. Add to dry ingredients. Mix lightly with no more than 25 strokes, just to moisten (overmixing causes tunnels).
3. Fill greased muffin pan wells two thirds full.
4. Bake at 400°F 25 to 30 minutes, or until done.

12 muffins

Beer Batter for Fritters

1 cup all-purpose flour
1 teaspoon baking powder
1 egg
1 cup beer
¼ cup vegetable oil
Deep fat for frying

1. Mix flour and baking powder. Add egg, beer, and oil. Beat until smooth.
2. Dip chunks of food (see below) into batter. Fry in 3 to 4 inches of fat at 375°F until golden brown. Drain on paper toweling.
3. Sprinkle fruit fritters with confectioners' sugar or top with Beer Dessert Sauce (page 76).

Note: Frozen foods should be completely thawed and dried thoroughly before frying.

Suggested foods for batter frying: Fish fillets, shrimp, oysters, scallops, cooked meat chunks, cubed ham, cubed cheese, cooked cauliflowerets, onion rings, zucchini strips or slices, mushrooms, quartered bananas, apple slices or rings, halved pineapple slices, apricot halves, strawberries, mandarin orange sections.

Soft Pretzels

A delicious nibbler to serve along with steins of foamy beer. Pretzels originated centuries ago in Germany.

2 packages active dry yeast
2 cups warm water (105° to 115°F)
½ cup sugar
¼ cup butter or margarine
1 egg
2 teaspoons salt
6½ to 7 cups all-purpose flour
1 egg yolk
2 tablespoons water
Coarse salt

1. In a large bowl, dissolve yeast in 2 cups warm water. Add sugar, butter, egg, 2 teaspoons salt, and 3 cups flour. Beat until smooth.
2. Stir in enough additional flour to form a stiff dough. Cover tightly with foil; refrigerate 2 to 24 hours.
3. Turn dough out onto a lightly floured board. Divide dough in half. Cut each half into 16 equal pieces. Roll each piece into a 20-inch length. Shape into looped pretzels (see illustration).
4. Place pretzels on lightly greased cookie sheets. Blend egg yolk and 2 tablespoons water; brush over pretzels. Avoid dripping on cookie sheet. Cover and let rise in a warm place until double in bulk (about 30 minutes).
5. Bake at 400°F 10 to 15 minutes, or until golden brown. Cool on wire racks.

32 pretzels

Cooking With Beer

Most of the major European beer-producing and beer-consuming countries seem to have one or more beer soups in their traditional national cuisine. Germany, Czechoslovakia, Lithuania, Belgium, England, the Scandinavian countries, and others all make beer soups which vary from the thick, porridge-like Ollebrod of Denmark to thin, sweetened beer soups that are almost like drinks.

Beer soups haven't caught on widely in the United States, but that's no reason for you to miss out on these taste-treats. Not all the beer soups are old European recipes either; some are of more recent invention. Some beer soups are quick and easy; some are slow-cooking varieties. Some are hearty main dishes; others are meant only to begin a meal. Turn to the menu section for German Beer Soup, Scandinavian Fruit Soup (really a dessert), and Easy Beer-Cheese Soup.

English Beer Soup

An old-time soup that could be served in mugs, if you prefer. It's warming on cold winter days.

3 cans or bottles (12 ounces each)
    beer or ale
¼ cup sugar
½ teaspoon grated lemon peel
3 tablespoons lemon juice
1 cinnamon stick
    Dash salt
¼ cup flour
2 tablespoons water

1. In a saucepan, combine beer, sugar, lemon peel, juice, cinnamon, and salt. Heat slowly, but do not boil.
2. Mix flour with water to form a paste. Stir into soup. Cook, stirring constantly, until slightly thickened.

About 1 quart; 4 servings

Czech Beer Soup *(Pivni Polevka)*

A thin soup that tastes like a hot beer nog.

1 can or bottle (12 ounces) beer
1½ cups water
2 tablespoons sugar
1 tablespoon butter
¼ teaspoon salt
2 egg yolks
½ cup half-and-half or cream

1. In a saucepan, combine beer, water, sugar, butter, and salt. Heat just to boiling.
2. Beat egg yolks until thick and lemon colored; beat in half-and-half. Add some of hot mixture; pour back into saucepan. Heat, stirring constantly, for a few minutes. Do not boil. Serve in soup cups.

3 cups; 3 or 4 servings

Danish Beer and Bread Soup *(Ollebrod)*

This very old, popular Danish dish is not strictly a soup, but is more the consistency of hot cooked cereal. It is served for breakfast with cream plus cinnamon and sugar on top. Or serve it for supper with a platter of cold cuts, salad, and pickles.

½ pound dark Danish rye bread
    or pumpernickel,
    torn in pieces
2 cups water
1 can or bottle (12 ounces) dark
    beer
¼ cup sugar
    Grated peel of ½ lemon
1 tablespoon lemon juice
1 cinnamon stick

1. Soak the bread in water and beer overnight. Purée in a blender.
2. Add remaining ingredients. Cook over low heat to the consistency of cooked cereal (10 to 15 minutes).
3. Pour into cereal bowls. Top with **cream** or **milk,** plus **cinnamon** and **sugar.**

4 to 6 servings

Note: If using light beer, add 1 teaspoon molasses.

Lithuanian Beer and Poppy Seed Soup
(Alaus su Agunom Sriuba)

This unusual Eastern European soup is thin—more like a hot beverage.

1 cup boiling water
⅓ to ½ cup poppyseed
2 cans or bottles (12 ounces each) beer
3 tablespoons honey
4 lemon slices
Rye croutons

1. Pour boiling water over poppy seed. Let stand 15 minutes. Crush with mortar and pestle, or process in a blender.
2. In a saucepan, combine beer, honey, and poppyseed mixture. Heat, but do not boil.
3. Serve in bowls or cups, topped with lemon slices and rye croutons.

About 4 cups; 4 servings

Belgian Onion Soup

Just like French onion soup, except that beer replaces part of the stock.

2 large red onions, sliced
6 tablespoons butter or margarine
3 cups chicken stock
1 can or bottle (12 ounces) beer
¼ teaspoon salt
¼ teaspoon pepper
4 to 6 thick slices French bread
Grated Parmesan cheese

1. In a large saucepan, sauté onion in butter until soft.
2. Add chicken stock, beer, salt, and pepper. Cover and simmer about 30 minutes. Adjust seasonings.
3. Broil bread on one side about 3 inches from heat. Turn; sprinkle generously with Parmesan cheese. Broil 1 to 2 minutes more, or until lightly browned.
4. Pour soup into bowls. Add cheese-covered bread.

4 cups; 4 to 6 servings

Cheese and Vegetable Soup with Beer

A light soup which makes a pleasing first course for a dinner party. Or serve it with small sandwiches for lunch.

1 large onion, finely chopped
1 large celery stalk, finely chopped
1 large carrot, finely chopped
6 cups chicken stock
½ cup butter or margarine
¾ cup flour
1½ cups milk
1 can or bottle (12 ounces) beer
½ pound Cheddar cheese, shredded (2 cups)
½ cup minced parsley
Salt and white pepper

1. Simmer onion, celery, and carrot in 2 cups stock until tender (about 20 minutes).
2. In a large soup pot, melt butter; stir in flour. Gradually stir in remaining stock. Add milk, beer, and vegetables with stock.
3. Cook, stirring constantly, until slightly thickened.
4. Just before serving, add cheese. Cook slowly, stirring, until melted. Stir in parsley. Season to taste with salt and pepper.

About 10 cups

Caraway-Cabbage Soup

3 tablespoons butter or margarine
1 head (2 pounds) cabbage,
    coarsely chopped
5 cups chicken stock
1 teaspoon caraway seed
¼ teaspoon pepper
1 can or bottle (12 ounces) beer
⅓ cup flour
1 cup cream, half-and-half, or
    milk
    Salt

1. Melt butter; add cabbage. Cook slowly, stirring often, until limp.
2. Add stock, caraway seed, and pepper. Cover and simmer about 1 hour, adding beer during last 10 minutes.
3. Mix flour and a little cream to a smooth paste; add remaining cream. Stir into soup. Cook, stirring constantly, until bubbly and slightly thickened. Season to taste with salt.

12 cups; 8 to 12 servings

Seashore Beer Soup

This easy soup becomes a palate-pleasing introduction to a sit-down dinner party.

1 can (10¾ ounces) condensed
    tomato soup
1 can (11 ounces) condensed
    green pea soup
1 can or bottle (12 ounces) beer
¼ teaspoon garlic salt
1 can (4½ ounces) tiny shrimp
1 cup half-and-half or cream

1. Place condensed soups in saucepan; stir in beer. Add garlic salt.
2. Heat to simmering, stirring until smooth. Simmer 3 to 4 minutes.
3. Just before serving, add undrained shrimp and half-and-half. Heat to serving temperature; do not boil.

6 servings

Quick Canned Soup with a Zest

1 can (10½ ounces) condensed
    meat and vegetable soup, any
    flavor
⅔ cup beer
⅔ cup water

Combine ingredients in a saucepan; heat to simmering. Simmer 2 to 3 minutes.

2⅔ cups; 2 servings

Easy Franks and Bean Soup

1 can (16 ounces) franks and
    beans
1 can or bottle (12 ounces) beer
¼ cup ketchup

Combine ingredients in a saucepan; heat to simmering. Simmer 2 to 3 minutes.

3½ cups; 3 servings

Note: **1 can (16 ounces) pork and beans** may also be used; add **2 frankfurters, sliced.**

Farm-Style Leek Soup

2 large leeks (1 pound) with part of green tops, sliced
2 medium onions, sliced
1 large garlic clove, minced
¼ cup butter or margarine
4 cups chicken stock or bouillon
2 cups uncooked narrow or medium noodles (3 ounces)
1 can or bottle (12 ounces) beer
1½ cups shredded semisoft cheese (Muenster, brick, process, etc.)
Salt and pepper

1. Cook leek, onion, and garlic in butter for 15 minutes, using low heat and stirring often.
2. Add stock. Cover and simmer 30 minutes.
3. Add noodles. Cover and simmer 15 minutes, or until noodles are tender.
4. Add beer; heat to simmering. Gradually add cheese, cooking slowly and stirring until melted. Season to taste with salt and pepper.

6 servings, about 1½ cups each

Savory Lentil Soup

A hearty main-dish soup for chilly days. Complete the menu with a fruit and cottage cheese salad plus dark rye bread. Or serve a tossed salad with cheese and fruit for dessert. Cheese cake is another dessert possibility.

1 pound dried lentils
6 cups water
1 to 1½ pounds smoked pork hocks; or 1 ham bone plus some diced ham
1 teaspoon thyme
1 bay leaf
1 medium onion, chopped
2 celery stalks, chopped
3 medium carrots, sliced
2 cans or bottles (12 ounces each) beer

1. In a large kettle combine lentils, water, pork hocks, thyme, and bay leaf. Cover and simmer 2 hours.
2. Add onion, celery, carrots, and beer. Cover and simmer 30 minutes more, or until tender.
3. Remove rind, fat, and meat from bones. Dice meat; add to soup. Add water if soup is too thick.

About 2½ quarts; 8 to 10 servings

Corny Beef Soup

A delicious made-from-scratch soup to serve as a main dish for dinner, supper, or lunch.

1 pound ground beef
1 medium onion, chopped
1 can (10¾ ounces) condensed tomato soup
1½ cups water
1 can (16 ounces) corn (undrained)
1 cup uncooked narrow noodles
1 can or bottle (12 ounces) beer
1 can (4 ounces) mushrooms (undrained), optional

1. Brown beef and onion; pour off drippings.
2. Add remaining ingredients, except beer and mushrooms. Cover and simmer 20 minutes.
3. Add beer and mushrooms. Cover and simmer 10 minutes more, or until noodles are tender. Add a little more water, if desired.

About 10 cups; 6 to 8 servings

Hearty Beef-Noodle Soup

This is a filling soup to serve for dinner on cold winter days. It's even better when topped with Caraway Dumplings.

2 pounds very meaty beef bones
  (plus some stew meat, if
  desired)
8 to 10 cups water
1 large onion, chopped
  Tops and leaves of 4 or 5
  celery stalks
2 teaspoons salt
½ teaspoon thyme or savory
¼ teaspoon pepper
2 garlic cloves, minced
2 bay leaves
1½ cups uncooked narrow noodles
1 can or bottle (12 ounces) beer
½ to ¾ cup frozen peas
½ recipe Caraway Dumplings
  (page 29) (optional)

1. In a large soup kettle, place bones with meat, 8 cups water, onion, celery, and seasonings. Cover and simmer 2 to 3 hours, or until meat is very tender.
2. Remove meat from bones; dice in small pieces. Return to soup.
3. Add uncooked noodles, beer, and peas. Heat to boiling. Add more water, if needed. If preparing dumplings, drop 6 spoonfuls batter onto boiling soup. Cover, reduce heat, and steam for 15 minutes; do not peek.

6 servings, about 1½ cups each

CHEESE and EGGS

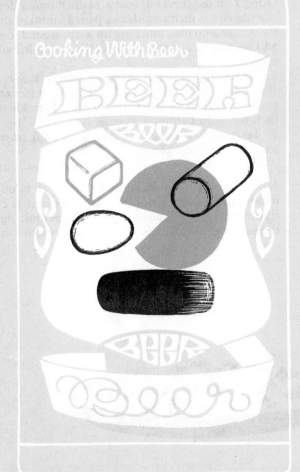

Cooking With Beer

BEER

Beer and cheese are perfect flavor companions, and so are beer and eggs. The internationally famous Welsh Rabbit is little more than melted Cheddar cheese thinned with beer. Cheese fondue can be made with beer, too, as Dutch Fondue. Or try a beer-flavored cheese strata, a puffy cheese-beer soufflé, or a superb homemade deep-pan pizza. Other cheese and beer recipes appear in the chapters on appetizers, breads, soups, and sauces.

The egg-and-beer recipes here are brunch and light-meal entrées. For other egg-and-beer combinations, refer to the dessert and beverage sections.

Beer Drinker's Deep-Pan Pizza

Beer is such a delicious and natural accompaniment for pizza, so why not put beer in the pizza, too? In this recipe it goes into the crust and the tomato sauce. This superb; extrathick pizza has come to be known as "Chicago-style."

Crust:
   1 cup warm beer (110° to 120°F)
   4 tablespoons olive or salad oil
   1 tablespoon sugar
1½ teaspoons salt
   1 package active dry yeast
2¾ to 3¼ cups all-purpose flour
   2 tablespoons cornmeal

Topping:
10 to 12 ounces mozzarella cheese, shredded or thinly sliced
   1 can (6 ounces) tomato paste
½ cup beer
   2 teaspoons oregano
   1 teaspoon fennel seed (optional)
½ teaspoon sugar
¾ to 1 pound bulk pork or Italian sausage, broken up
½ cup grated Parmesan cheese

1. For crust, combine in a large bowl the warm beer, 2 tablespoons oil, sugar, salt, and yeast. Add 1½ cups flour; beat until smooth. Stir in enough additional flour to make a fairly stiff dough.
2. Turn dough out onto a lightly floured surface. Knead until smooth and elastic (about 5 minutes). Place dough in a greased bowl, turning once to grease top. Cover and let rise in warm place (85°F) until double in bulk (about 1 hour).
3. Punch dough down. (For 2 small pizzas, divide in half.) Using 2 tablespoons oil, coat a 14-inch round deep pizza pan. (Or use two 9-inch round cake pans.) Sprinkle with cornmeal. Pat dough into pan, pinching up a rim around the edge. Cover and let rise in a warm place until double in bulk (about 30 minutes).
4. For topping, mix tomato paste, beer, oregano, fennel seed, and sugar. Cover pizza dough evenly with mozzarella cheese; evenly spoon on tomato paste mixture. Sprinkle with sausage, then top with Parmesan cheese.
5. Bake at 450°F 15 to 20 minutes, or until crust is browned and sausage is cooked.

One large or 2 small pizzas; 4 servings

Note: Alternate toppings could be (1) **1 can (4 ounces) sliced mushrooms,** drained, or (2) **8 anchovies** plus ⅓ cup chopped **ripe olives,** or (3) ½ **pound sliced pepperoni.** Omit or reduce the sausage, but include cheeses and tomato sauce.

Cheddar-Beer Omelets

6 eggs
⅓ cup beer
¼ teaspoon salt
    Dash Tabasco
2 to 3 tablespoons butter or
    margarine
½ cup shredded Cheddar cheese

1. Beat eggs slightly with beer, salt, and Tabasco.
2. Melt about 1 tablespoon butter in a 6- or 8-inch skillet. Pour in one fourth of egg mixture. As edges of omelet begin to thicken, draw cooked portions toward center with spoon or fork to allow uncooked mixture to flow to bottom of skillet. Shake and tilt as necessary to aid flow of uncooked eggs. Do not stir.
3. When eggs no longer flow but surface is still moist, sprinkle 2 tablespoons cheese over one half of omelet. Fold in half carefully. Cook about 30 seconds more. Slide onto warm platter.
4. Repeat to make 4 omelets.

4 servings

Cheese Soufflé au Bière

Beer and cheese are delectable partners, so combine them in a soufflé. Serve as main dish for lunch or a light supper. It doesn't require a sauce, but if you wish, top servings with a creamy mushroom or green pea sauce.

6 tablespoons butter or margarine
⅓ cup flour
¾ teaspoon dry mustard
½ teaspoon salt
⅛ teaspoon paprika
1 can or bottle (12 ounces) beer
½ pound sharp Cheddar cheese,
    shredded
6 eggs, separated

1. Melt butter in a saucepan; blend in flour, mustard, salt, and paprika. Heat until bubbly.
2. Stirring constantly, gradually add beer and cook until thickened. Add cheese; stir rapidly until melted and blended.
3. Beat egg yolks until thick and lemon colored. Slowly spoon sauce into yolks, stirring briskly.
4. Beat egg whites until stiff but not dry. Stir a large spoonful of whites into yolk mixture to lighten. Then add yolk mixture to remaining whites, very gently folding with wire whip or whisk.
5. Turn into a buttered and floured 2-quart soufflé dish.
6. Bake at 325°F 50 to 60 minutes, or until lightly browned and puffed.

6 servings

Beery Cheese Strata

Cut into squares and serve this dish as a pleasing entrée for brunch, lunch, or light supper. Accompany with link sausages.

12 slices day-old white bread
½ pound Cheddar cheese,
    shredded (2 cups)
2 tablespoons finely minced
    onion
4 eggs, slightly beaten
1 can (13 fluid ounces)
    evaporated milk
1 can or bottle (12 ounces) beer
½ cup water
2 teaspoons prepared mustard
1 teaspoon salt
⅛ teaspoon pepper

1. Trim crusts from bread. Arrange 6 slices in a buttered 2-quart rectangular baking dish (about 11x7 inches).
2. Cover bread with half the cheese and all the onion. Add remaining bread, then remaining cheese.
3. Mix eggs, milk, beer, water, mustard, salt, and pepper. Pour over bread and cheese. Add a little water if liquid doesn't reach top of bread.
4. Refrigerate overnight, or a minimum of 2 hours.
5. Bake at 325°F 50 minutes, or until set and lightly browned. Let stand 15 to 20 minutes before cutting into squares for serving.

8 servings

Welsh Rabbit

Welsh Rabbit is a centuries-old dish of cheese and beer or ale. It is sometimes called "rarebit," but this is incorrect. The addition of eggs to Welsh Rabbit turns it into a Golden Buck. Serve it for lunch, brunch, or a light supper.

1	tablespoon butter or margarine
1	pound Cheddar cheese, shredded
1	teaspoon dry mustard
½	teaspoon Worcestershire sauce
	Dash white pepper
¾	cup beer or ale
12	slices toast, halved diagonally

1. Melt butter in top of a double boiler.
2. Add cheese and seasonings. Cook, stirring occasionally, over boiling water until melted.
3. Gradually add beer. Cook, stirring, until smooth and hot.
4. For each serving, place 3 toast triangles on a plate. Top with about ⅓ cup sauce. If desired, sprinkle with paprika or top with tomato slices.

3 cups; 8 servings

Note: Welsh Rabbit may also be made at the table in a chafing dish. Be sure to use the bath of simmering water.

Golden Buck: Just before serving, add a little of the hot mixture to **2 beaten eggs.** Return to double-boiler top; cook, stirring constantly, over simmering water about 2 minutes.

Tomato Rabbit

A colorful variation of Welsh Rabbit.

1	tablespoon flour
⅓	cup beer
¼	teaspoon dry mustard
¼	teaspoon Worcestershire sauce
	Dash ground red pepper
2	cups shredded Cheddar cheese
1	medium tomato, peeled, seeded, and chopped
6	slices toast, halved diagonally

1. In a heavy saucepan, mix flour and a little beer to a smooth paste; add remaining beer and seasonings.
2. Add cheese. Cook over medium heat, stirring constantly, until melted and smooth.
3. Add tomato; stir until heated through. Serve immediately, allowing 3 toast halves and a scant ½ cup cheese mixture per serving. If desired, sprinkle with paprika.

4 servings

Savory Baked Eggs

This zesty egg dish is delicious at brunch, lunch, or a light supper. Each person gets two eggs in an individual ramekin; underneath is a bed of green peppers and onion, on top a crown of bread crumbs and cheese. The beer flavor does come through.

½	cup chopped green pepper (½ medium)
½	cup chopped onion (1 small)
1	small garlic clove, minced
1	tablespoon butter or margarine
4	eggs
¼	teaspoon salt
	Dash pepper
¼	cup fine dry bread or cracker crumbs
⅓	cup shredded Cheddar cheese
½	cup beer

1. Sauté green pepper, onion, and garlic in butter until soft. Spread in 2 ramekins or individual baking dishes.
2. Carefully break 2 eggs into each. Sprinkle with salt and pepper, then with mixture of crumbs and cheese. Pour beer over all.
3. Bake at 375°F 20 minutes, or until eggs are set.

2 servings

Eggs, Alsatian Style *(Oeufs à l'Alsace)*

This beer-and-cheese-flavored egg dish has the texture of very fluffy scrambled eggs.

6 eggs, separated
1 tablespoon minced onion
3 tablespoons butter or margarine
2 tablespoons minced fresh parsley
½ teaspoon salt
⅛ teaspoon pepper
⅛ teaspoon nutmeg
6 ounces semisoft cheese (Muenster, brick, etc.), shredded
1 cup beer
4 to 6 slices toast
4 to 6 anchovies (optional)

1. Beat egg whites until stiff but not dry.
2. In a large, heavy skillet (nonstick type preferred), sauté onion in butter; add parsley and seasonings.
3. Gradually add cheese and beer, cooking slowly and stirring until cheese melts.
4. Add a little hot mixture to egg yolks; return to skillet. Fold in beaten egg whites. Cook slowly and stir gently until mixture has consistency of fluffy scrambled eggs.
5. Serve on toast. Garnish with anchovies, if desired.

4 to 6 servings

Mushroom-Beer Soufflé

Serve as a side dish with steak or a roast. Or top with a cheese sauce and serve for lunch or a light supper.

⅓ cup minced green onion with tops, or yellow onion
⅓ cup butter or margarine
⅓ cup flour
1 can or bottle (12 ounces) beer
6 eggs, separated
¼ teaspoon sugar
½ teaspoon salt
  Dash ground red pepper
1 can (4½ ounces) mushroom stems and pieces, drained

1. Sauté onion in butter.
2. Stir in flour. Gradually add beer. Cook, stirring constantly, until thickened and smooth. Cool slightly.
3. Add egg yolks, one at a time, beating vigorously after each addition. Stir in seasonings and mushrooms.
4. Beat egg whites until stiff but not dry. Add yolk mixture; gently fold together until blended.
5. Turn into a buttered and lightly floured 2-quart soufflé dish. Run knife in a circle around mixture 1 inch from edge (to form "hat" on soufflé).
6. Bake at 325°F 50 to 60 minutes, or until knife comes out clean when inserted halfway between center and edge. Serve immediately.

8 side-dish servings;
4 to 6 main-dish servings

Dutch Fondue

This fondue is made with beer and a Dutch type of cheese, instead of the wine, kirsch, and Swiss cheese of the more familiar cheese fondue. The variation is quite tasty. Unsliced French-type white or rye bread, cut in chunks, could be used for dipping.

1 can or bottle (12 ounces) beer
1 tablespoon cornstarch
1 garlic clove, halved
12 ounces Edam or Gouda cheese
Dash white pepper
1 loaf unsliced French or rye bread (1 pound), cut in 1-inch cubes

1. Mix a little beer with cornstarch; set aside.
2. Rub inside of a nonmetal fondue pot with cut surface of garlic. Pour in beer; heat until beer is steaming and about to simmer (do not boil). If pot is ceramic, do not place on surface unit of range. Use candle warmer or follow manufacturer's directions.
3. Add cheese in small amounts, stirring constantly until melted. Blend in cornstarch mixture. Continue cooking and stirring about 5 minutes, or until fondue begins to bubble and is of desired thickness. Add pepper to taste.
4. Place bread cubes on fondue forks; dip in fondue. Keep fondue hot during dipping; otherwise it will become too thick.

4 to 6 servings

MEAT

In meat cookery beer is a classic ingredient. Used as a cooking liquid, it can enhance the finished dish in several ways. With slowly cooked meats, only a faint essence of beer remains, and a new, tantalizing blend of flavors emerges. When beer is added near the end of cooking, more of the characteristic beer flavor remains.

Beer makes a tangy marinade and will flavorfully penetrate meat if allowed to stand in the refrigerator overnight. Beer also becomes a distinctive basting sauce for roasts. If after cooking a roast or braised dish you prefer a little more pronounced beer taste, simply add additional beer to the gravy while it is being thickened.

Beer can be used regularly in family meat dishes, as well as adult party recipes, because the alcohol evaporates within the first few minutes of cooking. Meat dishes made with beer that appear in the menu section of this book are Irish Stew with Ale, German Pork Roast in Spicy Beer Sauce, Pork and Beans, Mexican Style, Chili with Beer, and Backyard Bratwurst in Beer for a Crowd.

Flemish Beef Stew (Carbonnade à la Flamande)

This world-famous dish of beef, beer, and onions is from Belgium. "Carbonnade" originally meant meat grilled over hot coals or embers, but in this dish it now means slow stewing. It makes a savory, guest-pleasing party dish for a buffet dinner. Spoon it over noodles and complete the menu with a tossed salad, French bread, cake, and steins of beer to drink.

　4　**pounds beef chuck or round, boneless, cut in 1-inch cubes**
　¼　**cup oil**
　2　**tablespoons parsley flakes**
　2　**teaspoons each thyme, sugar, and salt**
　½　**teaspoon pepper**
　2　**garlic cloves, minced**
　2　**bay leaves**
　2　**cans or bottles (12 ounces each) beer**
　8　**medium onions, sliced**
　¼　**cup cornstarch**

1. Brown meat in oil; place in a very large casserole or two medium ones, about 2½ quarts each. Add seasonings; stir to coat meat.
2. Add beer plus a little water, if needed, to almost cover meat. Cover casseroles.
3. Bake at 300°F 1½ hours.
4. Parboil onion half covered with water, stirring frequently, until soft. Stir into meat. Cover and continue baking 1 to 1½ hours, or until meat is tender.
5. Make a paste of cornstarch and a little water. Stir into casseroles. Return to oven about 10 minutes, stirring once or twice. Serve over **noodles.**

12 to 14 servings

Munich Beef

This German-style oven beef stew has a sweet-sour gravy.

　1　**can or bottle (12 ounces) beer**
　1　**medium onion, chopped**
　½　**teaspoon salt**
　⅛　**teaspoon pepper**
　1½　**pounds beef chuck, boneless, cut in 1-inch cubes**
　4　**medium carrots (¾ pound)**
　3　**tablespoons flour**
　2　**tablespoons currant or grape jelly**
　1　**tablespoon grated orange or lemon peel**
　1　**tablespoon lemon juice**
　4　**cups cooked noodles**

1. In a 2- to 2½-quart casserole, combine beer, onion, salt, and pepper. Add beef. Cover; marinate in refrigerator 10 to 24 hours, stirring occasionally.
2. Place casserole in oven (do not brown beef).
3. Bake at 300°F 1½ hours. Add carrots. Continue baking 1 hour longer, or until meat and carrots are tender.
4. Mix flour, jelly, peel, and lemon juice to a paste. Stir into stew. Bake 15 minutes more, stirring once or twice, until thickened and bubbly. Serve over noodles.

6 servings

Savory Beef Stew

Beer adds a subtle flavor to the gravy, although it is not a typical beer taste. The alcohol boils off early in the cooking, so the dish may be served to children.

1½ **pounds beef stew meat,
    boneless, cut in 1½-inch
    cubes**
¼ **cup flour**
1 **teaspoon salt**
¼ **teaspoon basil**
¼ **teaspoon savory or marjoram**
⅛ **teaspoon pepper**
3 **tablespoons vegetable oil**
2 **onions, sliced**
1 **can or bottle (12 ounces) beer**
½ **cup water**
1 **bay leaf**
5 **medium potatoes (1⅔ pounds)**
1 **pound carrots (8 to 10); or ½
    pound each parsnips and
    carrots**

1. Dredge meat in mixture of flour, salt, basil, savory, and pepper. Reserve excess flour. Brown meat in oil. Add onion, beer, water, and bay leaf. Cover and simmer 1½ hours.
2. Pare potatoes; cut into large cubes. Slice carrots and/or parsnips. Add vegetables to stew. If necessary, add a little more water.
3. Cover and simmer 1 hour more, or until meat and vegetables are tender. Make smooth paste of reserved flour mixture and a little water. Stir into stew during last 10 minutes of cooking.

6 servings

Sausage-Stuffed Rouladen with Tomato-Beer Kraut

1 **beef round steak, cut ½ inch
    thick (about 2 pounds)
    Flour**
6 **smoked link sausages**
2 **tablespoons oil**
2 **medium onions, sliced**
1 **can (16 ounces) sauerkraut,
    rinsed and drained**
1 **can (16 ounces) tomatoes
    (undrained)**
1 **can or bottle (12 ounces) beer**
2 **teaspoons caraway seed**
1 **teaspoon salt**
¼ **teaspoon pepper**
3 **tablespoons flour**

1. Cut beef into 6 serving pieces approximately rectangular in shape. Dredge in flour. Pound on a floured board until as thin as possible. Roll each piece around a sausage. Fasten with wooden picks.
2. In a large skillet, brown meat in oil; set aside. Sauté onion in same skillet until golden.
3. Add sauerkraut, undrained tomatoes, beer, caraway seed, salt, and pepper. Stir. Add beef rolls. Cover and simmer 1½ to 2 hours, or until tender.
4. Transfer meat and vegetables to a serving platter, using slotted spoon. Make paste of flour and a little water; stir into cooking liquid. Cook, stirring constantly, until thickened. Pass gravy in sauceboat.

6 servings

Scandinavian Sailors' Beef Casserole

This dish is frequently served in Scandinavian homes during the winter. It is a time-honored favorite among sailors.

1½ to 2 pounds beef round steak,
    boneless, cut ½ inch thick
    Flour
3 medium onions, sliced
¼ cup margarine, oil, or butter
6 medium potatoes, pared and
    thickly sliced
1 teaspoon salt
¼ teaspoon pepper
1 can or bottle (12 ounces) beer
¼ cup minced parsley (optional)

1. Cut meat into 6 serving pieces. Dredge in flour. Pound to ¼-inch thickness.
2. Sauté onion in 2 tablespoons margarine in a large skillet; set aside.
3. In remaining margarine, brown meat on both sides in same skillet.
4. In a large casserole, layer meat, potatoes, and onion, sprinkling layers with salt and pepper.
5. Pour beer into skillet; stir up brown bits. Add to casserole.
6. Cover and bake at 350°F 1½ hours, or until meat is tender. Sprinkle with parsley. Serve with **pickled beets.**

6 servings

Bachelor's Steak

A perfect main dish for an intimate dinner for two. Complete the menu with a green vegetable or salad, plus your choice of baked potatoes, white and wild rice, or french-fried potatoes (frozen for ease of preparation). Dessert could be ice cream topped with a liqueur.

2 small single-serving steaks (rib,
    rib eye, strip, T-bone)
1 garlic clove, halved
1 can (2 to 2½ ounces) sliced
    mushrooms
¼ to ⅓ cup beer
1 tablespoon flour
¼ teaspoon salt
    Dash pepper

1. Rub meat with cut surface of garlic. Broil 2 to 3 inches from heat until as done as desired.
2. Meanwhile, drain mushroom liquid into measuring cup. Add enough beer to measure ⅔ cup total liquid.
3. Pour 2 tablespoons steak drippings into a saucepan; stir in flour, salt, and pepper until smooth. Stir in beer mixture. Cook, stirring constantly, until thickened and smooth. Add drained mushrooms; heat through.
4. Pour beer-mushroom sauce over steak and **potatoes.**

2 servings

English Meat Patties

Similar to Salisbury steaks, this dish is flavored with beer.

1 pound ground beef
½ cup fine dry bread crumbs
½ cup beer
1 small onion, finely minced
½ teaspoon salt
    Dash pepper and garlic powder
    Oil
Gravy:
2 tablespoons drippings
2 tablespoons flour
½ cup beer
½ cup water
1 teaspoon Worcestershire sauce
¼ teaspoon salt
    Dash pepper

1. Combine beef, crumbs, beer, onion, salt, and pepper. Shape into 4 patties.
2. Pan-fry in a very small amount of oil in a skillet, pouring off drippings as they accumulate. Turn once, carefully, and cook until as done as desired. Place patties on a platter; keep warm.
3. For gravy, pour off drippings from skillet; return 2 tablespoons. Stir in flour. Add beer; stir until smooth. Add water and seasonings. Cook, stirring constantly, until thickened; stir up brown bits. After gravy boils, reduce heat and simmer 2 to 3 minutes to mellow beer flavor.

4 servings

Brewerburgers: Follow recipe for English Meat Patties; omit gravy. If desired, broil or grill over coals.

Mushroom-Beer Steaks

1 beef round steak, cut ½ inch
thick (2 pounds)
Flour for dredging
¼ cup shortening or cooking oil
2 large onions, sliced
2 garlic cloves, minced
1 can or bottle (12 ounces) beer
1 cup beef broth (homemade,
canned, or from bouillon
cubes)
¼ cup ketchup
½ teaspoon salt
¼ teaspoon pepper
1 bay leaf
1 can (4½ ounces) mushroom
stems and pieces
¼ cup flour

1. Cut meat into 6 serving pieces. Pound with meat mallet.
2. Dredge meat in flour. Brown in shortening in a large skillet; set meat aside.
3. Add onion and garlic to skillet, adding more fat if needed. Sauté until golden. Remove.
4. To skillet add beer, broth, ketchup, salt, pepper, and bay leaf. Stir up brown bits.
5. Layer meat and onions in skillet. Cover and simmer 1 to 1½ hours, or until meat is tender. Drain mushrooms, reserving liquid. Add mushrooms during last 5 minutes.
6. Place meat, onions, and mushrooms on serving platter; cover with foil to keep warm. Measure liquid. If needed, add water to measure about 2 cups.
7. Mix ¼ cup flour, mushroom liquid, and just enough water to make a smooth paste. Stir into cooking liquid. Cook, stirring constantly, until thickened. Serve gravy over meat and a **noodle** or **potato** accompaniment.

6 servings

Marinated Venison in Cream Gravy

This marinade may be used for various kinds of game: rabbit, duck, and other birds. Cut proportions, if necessary.

1 venison roast, preferably from
leg (4 to 5 pounds)
1 cup chopped onion
⅓ cup oil
2 cans or bottles (12 ounces each)
beer
2 tablespoons lemon juice
2 teaspoons salt
1 teaspoon thyme
8 peppercorns
2 garlic cloves, minced
1 bay leaf
½ cup cream or half-and-half
(about)
Flour

1. Place venison in a large glass bowl.
2. Sauté onion in oil. Stir in beer and seasonings. Pour over venison. Marinate in refrigerator 24 to 36 hours, turning occasionally.
3. Place venison and marinade in a Dutch oven. Cover.
4. Bake at 325°F 2½ hours, or until tender, basting several times. (Venison may be cooked a shorter time to rare, only if meat is from a young animal.)
5. Transfer venison to a platter. Strain cooking liquid; skim off most of fat. Measure liquid. Make a paste of cream and 2 tablespoons flour for each 1 cup cooking liquid. Combine the paste in a saucepan with liquid and cook, stirring constantly, until thickened. Season to taste. Serve in a sauceboat along with venison.

2 or 3 servings per pound

Old-World Short Ribs

Select meaty beef short ribs for this hearty and savory entrée. Serve with noodles, pouring gravy over both. Complete the meal with tossed salad, beverage, and dessert.

3 to 4 pounds beef short ribs
2 tablespoons oil
1 medium onion, chopped
1 can (8 ounces) tomato sauce
1 can or bottle (12 ounces) beer
1 teaspoon caraway seed
½ teaspoon salt
⅛ teaspoon pepper
1 bay leaf
¼ cup flour
2 to 3 cups cooked noodles

1. Brown ribs slowly in oil in a Dutch oven or deep skillet. Remove as they are browned.
2. Add onion and sauté until golden. Add tomato sauce, 1¼ cups beer, and seasonings. Return ribs.
3. Cover and simmer 1½ hours, or until tender.
4. Place ribs on platter; keep warm. Skim fat from cooking liquid (there should be about 2 cups liquid). Stir in paste made from flour and remaining ¼ cup beer. Cook, stirring constantly, until thickened. Serve gravy over ribs and noodles.

4 servings

Caraway Meat Loaf

With this meat loaf is a beer-flavored chili sauce to be poured over the slices.

1 pound ground beef
1 cup soft bread crumbs (from 2 slices white or rye bread)
1 small onion, minced
⅔ cup beer
1 egg
½ teaspoon caraway seed
½ teaspoon salt
¼ teaspoon pepper
⅓ cup chili sauce

1. Combine beef, crumbs, onion, ⅓ cup beer, egg, caraway seed, salt, and pepper.
2. Shape into a loaf. Place in a roasting pan. (Or pack into a 7 x 3½ x 2-inch loaf pan.)
3. Bake at 350°F 45 minutes.
4. Simmer chili sauce and remaining ⅓ cup beer about 5 minutes; serve over slices of meat loaf.

4 servings

Breaded Pork Chops with Beer Gravy

4 pork chops, cut ½ to ¾ inch thick
1 egg
1 tablespoon water
½ cup fine cracker crumbs (from about 12 saltines)
½ teaspoon salt
¼ teaspoon paprika
2 tablespoons oil
¾ cup beer
2 tablespoons flour
¾ cup beef bouillon
1 tablespoon ketchup

1. Dip chops in a mixture of egg and water, coating both sides. Mix crumbs, salt, and paprika. Dip egg-coated chops in this mixture, coating both sides well.
2. Brown chops slowly in oil, cooking about 15 minutes. Reduce heat; add ¼ cup beer. Cover and simmer 20 to 30 minutes, or until done.
3. Make a paste of flour and a little remaining beer. Place chops on platter. Stir flour paste, rest of beer, bouillon, and ketchup into cooking liquid. Cook, stirring constantly, until thickened. Season to taste, if desired. (Makes enough gravy to pour over meat and potatoes.)

4 servings

Jiffy Beer Chili *(Pronto Chili con Cerveza)*

A thick and savory chili that can be prepared in almost no time at all for cold days

½ pound ground beef
½ cup chopped onion (frozen, or 1 medium fresh)
1 can (6 ounces) tomato paste
1 can or bottle (12 ounces) beer
1 can (16 ounces) kidney beans (undrained)
1 to 1½ teaspoons chili powder
1 teaspoon sugar
1 teaspoon garlic salt
½ teaspoon oregano

1. Lightly brown ground beef and onion in a heavy medium saucepan; cook until onion is soft.
2. Add tomato paste and beer; stir up brown bits.
3. Add remaining ingredients. Cook slowly uncovered 10 to 15 minutes, or until onion is tender. Add a little water, if needed.

5 cups; 4 servings

Applesauce-Topped Beef and Sausage Loaf

Meat Loaf:
1 pound ground beef
½ pound pork sausage
½ cup dry bread or cracker crumbs
½ cup beer
1 small onion, minced
1 egg, slightly beaten
½ teaspoon salt
¼ teaspoon each sage, thyme, and garlic powder
⅛ teaspoon pepper

Topping and Sauce:
1⅓ cups applesauce
¼ cup beer

1. For meat loaf, mix ingredients. Shape into an elongated loaf. Place in a shallow roasting pan.
2. Bake at 350°F 50 minutes.
3. Spoon fat from pan. Spread ⅓ cup applesauce over meat loaf. Bake 10 minutes longer.
4. For sauce, heat 1 cup applesauce and beer to simmering; serve over meat loaf slices.

6 servings

Bavarian Casserole

A good use for leftover roast pork.

2 celery stalks, chopped
1 medium onion, chopped
3 tablespoons butter or margarine
½ teaspoon salt
¼ teaspoon sage
¼ teaspoon sugar
⅛ teaspoon pepper
1 cup beer
4 cups pumpernickel bread cubes (5 slices)
2 cups cubed cooked pork (10 ounces)

1. Sauté celery and onion in butter until soft; stir in seasonings. Add beer.
2. Place bread and pork in a 1½-quart casserole. Add beer-vegetable mixture. Stir lightly.
3. Cover and bake at 375°F 30 to 35 minutes.

4 servings

Savory Spareribs

4 pounds pork spareribs
1 can or bottle (12 ounces) beer
½ cup honey
2 tablespoons lemon juice
2 teaspoons salt
1 teaspoon dry mustard
¼ teaspoon pepper

1. Cut spareribs into 2-rib sections.
2. Combine remaining ingredients in a shallow glass or ceramic baking dish. Add ribs. Marinate in refrigerator at least 24 hours, turning and basting occasionally.
3. Arrange ribs in a single layer in a large baking pan; reserve marinade.
4. Bake at 350°F 1½ hours, turning once and basting frequently with marinade.

4 to 6 servings

Lagered Ham and Noodle Casserole

Beer delicately flavors the cheese sauce in this delicious family-style casserole.

1 medium green pepper, chopped
1 medium onion, chopped
¼ cup butter or margarine
3 tablespoons flour
½ teaspoon dry mustard
½ teaspoon salt
Dash pepper
⅓ cup instant nonfat dry milk
1 can or bottle (12 ounces) beer
1 cup shredded Cheddar cheese
   (4 ounces)
8 ounces uncooked medium
   noodles, cooked and drained
2 cups diced cooked ham (⅔
   pound)

1. For sauce, slowly sauté green peeper and onion in butter until soft and almost tender. Stir in flour and seasonings.
2. Mix dry milk and ⅓ cup beer.
3. Gradually add remaining beer to flour mixture. Cook, stirring constantly, until thickened and bubbly. Add cheese; stir until melted. Remove from heat; add beer-milk mixture.
4. Combine sauce, cooked noodles, and ham. Turn into a 2½-quart casserole.
5. Bake at 350°F 20 minutes, or until heated through and bubbly.

6 servings

Orange-Ginger Lamb Chops

4 lamb leg sirloin or shoulder
   chops
1 tablespoon oil
¾ teaspoon salt
¼ teaspoon ginger
Dash pepper
1 orange, peeled
1 small to medium onion
1 can or bottle (12 ounces) beer
2 tablespoons sugar
1 tablespoon cornstarch

1. Brown chops in oil in a skillet; pour off fat. Mix salt, ginger, and pepper. Sprinkle over chops.
2. Cut off a thin slice from each end of orange. Cut remainder of orange into 4 slices. Remove seeds. Repeat with onion; do not separate into rings.
3. Top each chop with an orange slice, then an onion slice. Add 1¼ cups beer. Cover and simmer 30 minutes, or until meat is tender.
4. Transfer chops topped with orange and onion to a platter.
5. Mix sugar, cornstarch, and remaining ¼ cup beer. Add to liquid in skillet. Cook, stirring constantly, until thickened. Add dash of salt, if desired. Strain into a sauceboat. Accompany chops with rice, pouring sauce over both.

4 servings

Fruited Pork Roast, Scandinavian Style

Prunes and apple are stuffed inside a boneless pork roast to create an unusual entrée that's nice for a party or a special family meal. The slices are especially attractive. The sweetened sauce retains just a hint of beer flavor.

1 **pork rolled loin roast, boneless, (3 to 3½ pounds)**
8 to 10 **pitted dried prunes**
1 **can or bottle (12 ounces) beer**
½ **teaspoon ginger**
1 **medium apple, pared and chopped**
1 **teaspoon lemon juice**
½ **teaspoon salt**
Dash pepper
¼ **cup flour**

1. Make pocket down center of roast by piercing with a long, sharp tool such as a steel knife sharpener; leave strings on roast. (Alternate method: Remove strings. Using strong knife, cut pocket in pork by making a deep slit down length of loin, going to within ½ inch of the two ends and within 1 inch of other side.)
2. Meanwhile, combine prunes, beer, and ginger in a saucepan; heat to boiling. Remove from heat; let stand 30 minutes.
3. Mix apple with lemon juice to prevent darkening. Drain prunes, reserving liquid; pat dry with paper towels. Mix prunes and apple.
4. Pack fruit into pocket in pork, using handle of wooden spoon to pack tightly. (With alternate method of cutting pocket, tie with string at 1-inch intervals. Secure with skewers or sew with kitchen thread.)
5. Place meat on rack in a roasting pan.
6. Roast at 350°F 2 to 2½ hours, allowing 40 to 45 minutes per pound. During last 45 minutes of roasting, spoon fat from pan; baste occasionally with liquid drained from prunes.
7. Transfer meat to a platter. Skim fat from cooking liquid; measure liquid. Add a little water to roasting pan to help loosen brown bits; add to cooking liquid. Add salt, pepper, and enough additional water to measure 2 cups total. Make a paste of flour and a little more water. Combine with cooking liquid. Cook, stirring constantly, until thickened. Pass in a sauceboat for pouring over meat slices.

8 servings

Piquant Lamb Kabobs

Grill these colorful kabobs outdoors or broil inside. It's a year-round dish. If you wish, substitute tender beef cubes for the lamb.

1½ **pounds boneless lamb (leg or sirloin), cut in 1-inch cubes**
18 **fresh medium mushrooms (about ½ pound)**
¾ **cup beer**
1 **can (6 ounces) pineapple juice (¾ cup)**
2 **tablespoons oil**
2 **teaspoons soy sauce**
1 **garlic clove, quartered**
18 **cherry tomatoes (about 1 pint)**
18 **green pepper squares (1 large pepper)**
4 to 5 **cups cooked rice**

1. Place lamb cubes and whole mushrooms in a ceramic casserole.
2. Combine beer, pineapple juice, oil, soy sauce, and garlic. Pour over lamb and mushrooms. Add a little more beer, if needed.
3. Cover and refrigerate at least 6 hours, or overnight.
4. On each of 6 long skewers, alternate lamb cubes with mushrooms, cherry tomatoes, and green pepper squares. Use 3 each of the vegetables for each skewer.
5. Broil 3 inches from heat to desired doneness (about 10 to 15 minutes), turning once or twice. Watch that vegetables do not overcook.
6. Heat marinade to pass as sauce. Serve kabobs on or with rice.

6 servings

Sausage in Beer

1 can or bottle (12 ounces) beer
3 medium onions, thinly sliced
2 medium carrots, thinly sliced
1 teaspoon Worcestershire sauce
½ teaspoon salt
8 bratwurst, knockwurst, Polish sausage, or large frankfurters
8 frankfurter buns

1. Put beer, onion, carrot, Worcestershire sauce, and salt in a saucepan. Heat to boiling. Cover, reduce heat, and simmer 15 minutes.

2. Add sausage. Cover and simmer 15 minutes more, stirring occasionally.

3. Place sausages in buns. Using a slotted spoon, lift vegetables from liquid and place on sausages.

8 servings

Luxemburg Stew

2 pounds boneless veal shoulder or stew meat, cut in 1-inch cubes
⅓ cup flour
6 tablespoons butter or margarine
1 large onion, sliced
2 cans (16 ounces each) tomatoes, broken up
1 can or bottle (12 ounces) beer
6 whole cloves
1 teaspoon salt
½ teaspoon thyme
¼ teaspoon crushed rosemary
¼ teaspoon paprika
8 gingersnaps
2 tablespoons lemon juice

1. Dredge veal in flour. Brown in ¼ cup butter in a saucepot. Remove meat.

2. Add remaining 2 tablespoons butter and onion to saucepot. Sauté until golden.

3. Add veal, tomatoes with liquid, beer, and seasonings. Cover and simmer 1 hour.

4. Moisten gingersnaps with a little water; crush. Stir into meat. Simmer 5 minutes more. Add lemon juice; mix well.

5. Serve over **rice** or **noodles** or with **potatoes.**

8 servings

Note: Poultry or lean pork could be substituted for veal.

German Veal Chops

4 veal loin or rib chops
Butter or margarine
2 medium onions, sliced
1 cup dark beer
1 bay leaf
½ teaspoon salt
Dash pepper
2 tablespoons flour

1. Brown veal in butter in a skillet; set meat aside. Sauté onion in same skillet until golden.

2. Add beer, bay leaf, salt, and pepper. Cover and simmer 15 minutes.

3. Transfer veal and onion to a platter. Make a paste of flour and a little water; stir into cooking liquid in skillet. Cook, stirring constantly, until thickened and smooth. Pour over veal and onion.

4 servings

Note: If you do not have dark beer, add ½ **teaspoon molasses** to light beer.

POULTRY and FISH

Cooking With Beer

BEER

Cooking poultry and fish in beer is similar to cooking meat in beer. The beer flavor changes and becomes more subtle the longer the dish cooks. When added at the end to the gravy, an especially zesty taste results.

Beer is also a flavorful ingredient in batters for frying chicken and fish fillets. Beer is a tangy marinade liquid, too. Some of these recipes are for family meals; others make great company fare. Shrimp recipes are in the appetizer chapter.

Roast Chicken with Orange-Beer Sauce

1 roasting chicken (4 to 5 pounds)
Stuffing (optional)
Salt and pepper
1 can or bottle (12 ounces) beer
½ cup orange juice
2 tablespoons lemon juice
2 tablespoons tomato paste or ketchup
2 teaspoons sugar
¼ cup flour
Fresh parsley and orange slices

1. Stuff chicken, if desired; truss. Rub with salt and pepper. Place in a roasting pan.
2. Combine 1 cup beer, orange juice, lemon juice, tomato paste, and sugar. Pour a little over chicken.
3. Roast, uncovered, at 375°F 2 to 2½ hours, or until done, basting occasionally with remaining beer mixture.
4. Transfer chicken to platter; keep warm. Skim fat from drippings; measure remaining liquid. If needed, add water to make 1½ cups. Make paste with flour and remaining ½ cup beer. Combine with liquid. Cook, stirring constantly, until thickened. Season with salt and pepper to taste.
5. Garnish chicken with parsley and orange slices. Pass sauce to pour over slices after carving.

6 servings

Ham-Bread Stuffing for Chicken: Combine **3 cups fresh bread cubes, ¼ pound ground ham, 1 small onion, minced, 2 tablespoons melted butter, ½ teaspoon salt, ¼ teaspoon sage, a dash pepper,** and just enough **beer** to moisten.

Brewers' Chicken

You don't taste the beer in this creamy, smooth sauce, but it imparts a subtly savory flavor.

1 broiler-fryer chicken (2 to 2½ pounds), cut up
12 small white onions; or 3 medium onions, sliced
3 tablespoons cooking oil
¾ cup beer
1 tablespoon ketchup
½ teaspoon each thyme or rosemary, paprika, and salt
1 bay leaf
½ cup milk or half-and-half
3 tablespoons flour

1. In a large skillet, brown chicken and onions in oil, removing pieces as they brown. Pour off excess fat.
2. Add beer, ketchup, and seasonings to skillet. Stir up brown bits.
3. Return chicken and onions to skillet. Cover and simmer 30 to 35 minutes, or until tender.
4. With a slotted spoon, transfer chicken and onions to serving platter; keep warm. Boil down cooking liquid to about 1½ cups.
5. Stir milk into flour until smooth. Add to liquid in skillet. Cook, stirring constantly, until thickened and smooth. Strain, if desired.

4 servings

Broiled Marinated Chicken

Cook this chicken indoors in the broiler or outdoors over hot coals.

1 broiler-fryer chicken (2 to 2½
    pounds), cut up
1 can or bottle (12 ounces) beer
2 tablespoons lemon juice
2 tablespoons oil
2 tablespoons honey
1 garlic clove, slivered
½ teaspoon crushed rosemary
½ teaspoon salt
⅛ teaspoon pepper

1. Place chicken in a shallow dish just large enough to hold pieces. Combine remaining ingredients; pour over chicken. Marinate in refrigerator at least 6 hours or overnight.
2. Grill or broil 6 to 8 inches from heat, basting often with marinade and turning, 30 to 40 minutes, or until tender.

4 servings

African-Style Chicken

1 broiler-fryer chicken (2 to 2½
    pounds), cut up
2 tablespoons peanut or other
    cooking oil
1 medium onion, chopped
1 garlic clove, minced
¾ cup beer
⅓ cup ground peanuts
1 tablespoon lemon juice
1 tablespoon honey
½ teaspoon salt
¼ to ½ teaspoon dried ground
    chili pepper or chili powder
¼ teaspoon ginger
3 tablespoons cream or milk
2 to 3 tablespoons flour
¼ cup flaked coconut

1. Brown chicken in oil in a heavy skillet; set aside.
2. Sauté onion and garlic in same skillet until golden. Add beer, peanuts, lemon juice, honey, and seasonings; mix.
3. Return chicken to skillet. Cover and simmer 35 to 40 minutes, or until tender.
4. Place chicken on a platter; keep warm. Measure cooking liquid. Make a paste of cream and flour, using 2 tablespoons flour per 1 cup cooking liquid. Add coconut. Cook, stirring constantly, until thickened. Pour part of sauce over chicken. Pass remainder to pour over **rice** or **potatoes.**

4 servings

Chicken and Rice in Beer

Chicken, rice, and flavorings bake together in this meal-in-one casserole. Beer is used in place of water to cook the rice. Complete the dinner with a green salad and fruit or a custard dessert.

1 broiler-fryer chicken (2 to 2½
    pounds), cut up
2 tablespoons oil
2 medium onions, chopped
1 garlic clove, minced
¾ cup uncooked rice (not instant)
½ green pepper, chopped
½ cup chopped fresh or canned
    tomatoes
1½ teaspoons salt
¼ teaspoon pepper
1 can or bottle (12 ounces) beer
2 bay leaves

1. Brown chicken in oil in a large skillet; set chicken aside.
2. In same skillet, sauté onion and garlic until golden.
3. Stir in rice, green pepper, tomatoes, 1 teaspoon salt, and pepper. Put mixture into a large, shallow baking dish.
4. Sprinkle chicken with ½ teaspoon salt; place on top of rice mixture.
5. Add beer to skillet; stir up brown bits. Pour over chicken and vegetables. Add bay leaves.
6. Cover tightly with foil or lid.
7. Bake at 375°F 40 to 60 minutes, or until chicken and rice are tender.

4 servings

Crunchy Fried Chicken

Chicken is dipped in a beer batter, then fried. The resulting coating is tender, crisp, and so delicious!

1 cup all-purpose flour
½ teaspoon salt
¼ teaspoon pepper
2 eggs
½ cup beer
1 broiler-fryer chicken (2 to 2½ pounds), cut up
   Cooking oil

1. Mix flour, salt, and pepper. Beat eggs with beer; add to flour mixture. Stir until smooth.
2. Dip chicken in batter, coating pieces well. Chill 1 hour.
3. Fry chicken in hot oil ½ to 1 inch deep 15 minutes on one side. Turn; fry on other side 5 to 10 minutes, or until browned and done. Drain on absorbent paper.

4 servings

German Beer Fish (Bier Fisch)

This recipe is an old tradition in Germany. The sauce combines sweet, sour, and spicy flavors. In Germany, fresh carp would be used, but since good fresh carp is hard to find in this country, other fish may be substituted. It should not be too delicate in flavor.

1 whole carp, buffalo fish, or pike (2 to 3 pounds with head); or 1 to 1½ pounds boneless fillets
2 tablespoons butter or margarine
1 medium onion, chopped
1 celery stalk, chopped
½ teaspoon salt
6 peppercorns
3 whole cloves
4 slices lemon
1 bay leaf
1 can or bottle (12 ounces) beer
6 gingersnaps, crushed
1 tablespoon sugar
   Fresh parsley for garnish

1. Remove head from fish; discard or use to make fish stock for other recipes. Lay fish out as flat as possible, breaking bones along back.
2. Melt butter in a skillet. Add onion, celery, salt, peppercorns, and cloves; mix. Top with lemon slices and bay leaf. Place fish on top.
3. Add beer. Cover and simmer 15 to 20 minutes, or just until fish flakes with a fork. Transfer fish to a platter; cover with foil to keep warm.
4. Strain cooking liquid, pressing some of vegetables through.
5. Put gingersnaps and sugar in skillet; stir in 1½ cups strained liquid. Cook, stirring constantly, until thickened.
6. Garnish fish with fresh parsley. Pass sauce for pouring over fish and **boiled potato** accompaniment.

4 to 6 servings

Beer-Batter Fried Sole

The batter for this fried fish dish is light and crisp with a delicate beer flavor. Other fish fillets may be substituted for the sole.

2 pounds fillet of sole (or any white-fleshed fish)
¾ cup flour
1 teaspoon baking powder
½ teaspoon onion powder (or 1 teaspoon onion salt, omitting salt)
½ teaspoon salt
⅛ teaspoon white pepper
½ cup beer
2 eggs, beaten
   Vegetable oil
   Tartar sauce

1. Thaw fish, if frozen. Pat dry with paper towels. Cut each piece in half lengthwise.
2. Combine flour, baking powder, and seasonings. Mix beer with eggs and 2 tablespoons oil; add to dry ingredients. Stir just until moistened.
3. Heat ¼ inch oil in a skillet. Dip each piece of fish in batter, coating well. Fry until golden brown on both sides. Serve with tartar sauce.

6 to 8 servings

Mock Lobster, Flemish Style

The main ingredient in this dish is monk fish, which has a taste and texture somewhat similar to lobster. Served in scallop shells or ramekins, it makes a delectable fish course during a multiple-course dinner

1 **pound monk fish fillets**
1 **can or bottle (12 ounces) beer**
½ **cup water**
1 **small onion, quartered**
1 **small celery stalk with top, cut in chunks**
½ **teaspoon salt**
¼ **teaspoon thyme**
2 **tablespoons butter or margarine**
2 **tablespoons flour**
¼ **cup cream**
1 **egg yolk**
½ **cup shredded cheese (Edam, Gruyère, Cheddar)**

1. Cut fish fillets in half lengthwise; then cut each section into ¾-inch slices.
2. In a large saucepan, place beer, water, onion, celery, salt, and thyme. Heat to boiling. Add fish. Cover and simmer 4 minutes, or until fish flakes.
3. Remove fish with a slotted spoon. Drain well on paper towels. Boil stock 10 minutes to reduce; strain.
4. In another saucepan, melt butter. Stir in flour. Add ¾ cup strained stock and the cream. Cook, stirring constantly, until thickened.
5. Add a little hot mixture to egg yolk; return to pan. Cook slowly, stirring, 1 to 2 minutes. Remove from heat; adjust seasonings.
6. Gently combine fish and sauce. Spoon into scallop shells or individual ramekins. Sprinkle with cheese. Broil 2 minutes, or just until tops are lightly browned.

6 appetizer servings

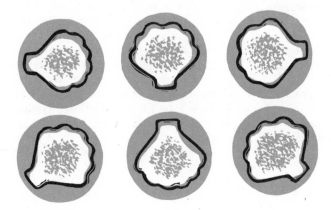

Saucy Fish Fillets

This delicately flavored entrée consists of fish poached in beer and a hollandaise-style sauce with egg yolks, cream, butter, and part of the cooking liquid.

1 **pound fish fillets**
1 **can or bottle (12 ounces) beer**
1 **small onion, quartered**
1 **celery stalk, cut in chunks**
2 **tablespoons minced fresh parsley or 1 tablespoon dried parsley flakes**
1 **teaspoon salt**
   Dash white pepper
2 **egg yolks**
2 **tablespoons cream**
2 **tablespoons butter or margarine**

1. Thaw fish, if frozen.
2. Put beer, onion, celery, parsley, salt, and pepper in a skillet. Heat to boiling. Add fish. Cover and simmer about 8 to 10 minutes, or just until fish flakes with a fork.
3. Drain fish and put onto a deep platter. Place in a 300°F oven to keep warm. Boil cooking liquid about 5 minutes to reduce; strain.
4. In top of a double boiler, beat egg yolks with cream. Gradually stir in ½ cup hot strained cooking liquid. Cook over boiling water, stirring constantly, until thickened. Cut butter into small pieces; stir into sauce, one piece at a time. Pour sauce over fish. (Recipe makes about ¾ cup sauce.)

3 or 4 servings

Tuna and Swiss Cheese Pie

3 eggs
½ teaspoon salt
½ teaspoon dry mustard
   Dash pepper
1 cup whipping cream or
   half-and-half
¾ cup ale or beer
1 unbaked 9-inch pastry shell,
   chilled
2 cans (6½ or 7 ounces each)
   tuna, drained and flaked
6 ounces Swiss cheese, shredded
1 tablespoon flour

1. Beat eggs, salt, dry mustard, and pepper until foamy. Beat in cream and ale.
2. Cover bottom of pastry shell with a layer of tuna. Sprinkle half of cheese over tuna. Repeat layering. Sprinkle flour over cheese. Pour egg mixture over all.
3. Bake at 425°F 15 minutes. Turn oven control to 300°F and bake 25 minutes, or until a knife inserted halfway between center and edge of filling comes out clean.

6 entrée servings;
10 to 12 appetizer servings

Tuna-Macaroni Bake

1 package (7¼ ounces) macaroni
   and cheese dinner
6 cups boiling water, salted
2 tablespoons butter or margarine
1 can or bottle (12 ounces) beer
¼ teaspoon salt
1 can (6½ or 7 ounces) tuna,
   drained and flaked
¼ cup chopped green pepper
1 canned pimento, chopped
⅓ cup instant nonfat dry milk
2 eggs, slightly beaten

1. Cook macaroni in boiling salted water in a large saucepan, stirring occasionally, until tender (about 7 to 10 minutes). Drain; return macaroni to pan.
2. Add butter, ½ cup beer, contents of cheese sauce packet from dinner, and salt. Stir until butter is melted. Add tuna, green pepper, and pimento. (Two pimentos or ½ cup chopped green pepper may be used instead of some of each, if desired.)
3. Turn into a lightly buttered rectangular 1½-quart baking dish. Combine remaining beer, dry milk, and eggs; pour over macaroni mixture.
4. Bake at 325°F 1½ hours, or until lightly browned on edges and set.

4 servings

SAUCES
and DRESSINGS

This chapter presents a variety of zesty beer recipes for serving over other foods. There are warm sauces to pour over cooked vegetables, meats, poultry, and fish. There are a few that can be used as basting sauces for roasts and grilled meats. Some sauces can become binders for casseroles. Others are sweet dessert sauces. Salad dressings can also be enhanced with beer. This chapter includes a dressing for shrimp, a few for vegetable and green salads, a few for fruit salads.

Herbed Tomato Sauce

Serve this tangy sauce with meat, poultry, fish, eggs, vegetables, or in casseroles.

1 **medium onion, chopped**
1 **garlic clove, minced**
1 **tablespoon oil**
1 **tablespoon minced fresh parsley**
2 **teaspoons sugar**
½ **teaspoon salt**
½ **teaspoon basil**
¼ **teaspoon oregano**
  Dash pepper
1 **can or bottle (12 ounces) beer**
1 **can (6 ounces) tomato paste**

1. Sauté onion and garlic in oil until soft. Stir in seasonings.
2. Add beer and tomato paste. Slowly simmer 25 to 30 minutes.

About 2 cups

Savory Barbecue Sauce

Serve with hamburgers or hot dogs. Or use as a basting sauce while broiling or grilling chicken, pork chops, or ribs.

1 **can or bottle (12 ounces) beer**
1 **cup chili sauce**
½ **cup molasses**
¼ **cup prepared mustard**
1 **medium onion, chopped**
  Dash each Worcestershire sauce, salt, and pepper

1. Put all ingredients into a saucepan. Simmer about 10 minutes. Add more beer or water if needed.
2. Store unused sauce in refrigerator.

3 to 3¼ cups

Brown Beer Sauce

Serve with leftover beef, pork, or turkey, or spoon on mashed potatoes.

3 **tablespoons butter or margarine**
3 **tablespoons flour**
1 **can or bottle (12 ounces) beer**
2 **beef bouillon cubes**
2 **teaspoons Worcestershire sauce**
  Dash pepper

1. In a medium saucepan, melt butter; stir in flour.
2. Add beer gradually while stirring. Add bouillon cubes, Worcestershire sauce, and pepper.
3. Cook, stirring constantly, until thickened. Continue cooking and stirring 1 minute longer.

About 1½ cups

Tangy Cheese Sauce

Serve hot on vegetables, poultry, or fish.

3 tablespoons butter or margarine
3 tablespoons flour
½ teaspoon dry mustard
¼ teaspoon sugar
Dash pepper
1 can or bottle (12 ounces) beer
⅓ cup grated Parmesan cheese or
½ cup shredded Cheddar
cheese

1. Melt butter; stir in flour, dry mustard, sugar, and pepper. Heat and stir until bubbly.
2. Stirring constantly, gradually add beer and cook until thickened.
3. Add cheese. Cook slowly, stirring, until melted.

About 1¾ cups

Creamy Beer-Cheese Sauce

This made-from-scratch, zesty cheese sauce is delicious in casseroles or served over vegetables. Or add tuna, leftover meat or poultry, or sliced frankfurters and serve over rice. Adding the milk at the end prevents possible curdling.

3 tablespoons butter or margarine
3 tablespoons flour
½ teaspoon dry mustard
½ teaspoon salt
Dash pepper
½ teaspoon Worcestershire sauce
⅓ cup instant nonfat dry milk
1 can or bottle (12 ounces) beer,
warm
1 cup shredded Cheddar cheese
(4 ounces)
2 tablespoons powdered nondairy
creamer

1. Melt butter; stir in flour and seasonings.
2. Mix dry milk with ⅓ cup beer. Gradually add remaining beer to flour mixture.
3. Cook, stirring constantly, until thickened and smooth. Add cheese and creamer; stir until melted.
4. Remove from heat; add milk mixture.

2 cups

Mustard Sauce

Serve this sauce hot with hot dogs, bratwurst, Polish sausage, ham, tongue, pot roast, or as a dunk for beef fondue.

2 tablespoons cornstarch
2 tablespoons sugar
1 tablespoon dry mustard
¼ teaspoon salt
1 can or bottle (12 ounces) beer
1 tablespoon vinegar

1. In a saucepan, combine cornstarch, sugar, dry mustard, and salt. Stir in beer and vinegar.
2. Cook, stirring constantly, until thickened and bubbly. Serve hot.

1½ cups

Mushroom Sauce

1 can (2 to 2½ ounces)
    mushrooms
¼ to ⅓ cup beer
2 tablespoons butter or pan
    drippings
1 tablespoon flour
¼ teaspoon salt
    Dash pepper

1. Drain mushrooms, reserving liquid. Add enough beer to liquid to measure ⅔ cup.
2. Melt butter in a saucepan; stir in flour, salt, and pepper.
3. Stirring constantly, add liquid gradually and cook until thickened and smooth. Serve over steaks or roasts.

About 1 cup

Beer-Raisin Sauce

3 tablespoons brown sugar
1 tablespoon cornstarch
¼ teaspoon salt
¼ teaspoon cloves
⅛ teaspoon cinnamon
    Few grains nutmeg
1 cup beer
½ cup seedless raisins
1 teaspoon lemon juice

1. Mix brown sugar, cornstarch, salt, and spices in a saucepan. Stir in beer and raisins.
2. Bring to boiling, stirring constantly; cook until thick and clear (about 3 minutes).
3. Remove from heat and stir in lemon juice.
4. Serve hot with **ham slices.**

1½ cups

Beer-Oil Salad Dressing

Like a standard French vinegar and oil dressing, except that beer replaces the vinegar. A piquant dressing for tossed green salads.

½ cup oil
⅓ cup beer
¼ teaspoon dry mustard
¼ teaspoon salt
⅛ teaspoon freshly ground pepper
    Dash garlic powder

Process ingredients in a blender or shake vigorously in a covered jar.

About ¾ cup

Poppyseed-Beer Salad Dressing

Delicious on fruit salads.

½ cup beer
½ cup oil
¼ cup honey
1 teaspoon poppyseed
1 teaspoon lemon juice
¼ teaspoon dry mustard
¼ teaspoon salt

Shake ingredients in a covered jar.

1¼ cups

Ginger-Beer Mayonnaise

1 cup mayonnaise
½ cup beer
1 teaspoon sugar
¼ teaspoon ginger

Mix ingredients until smooth and well blended.

1½ cups

Beer Dressing for Potato Salad

½ cup diced onion
3 tablespoons salad oil
2 tablespoons flour
2 teaspoons sugar
1 teaspoon salt
⅛ teaspoon pepper
1 can or bottle (12 ounces) beer
¼ cup vinegar

1. Sauté onion in oil about 10 minutes.
2. Blend in flour, sugar, salt, and pepper. Stirring constantly, gradually add beer and cook until thickened and bubbly. Reduce heat; simmer about 5 minutes.
3. Cool slightly. Pour over warm cubed potatoes for salad; chill.

1¾ cups dressing

Beer Dressing for Cole Slaw

1 cup mayonnaise or salad dressing
½ cup beer
2 tablespoons finely minced onion
1 teaspoon celery seed
½ teaspoon salt
Dash Tabasco

Combine ingredients. Chill 1 hour or more to blend flavors. Makes enough for 1 medium head cabbage, shredded.

About 1½ cups

Curried Dressing

1 cup mayonnaise
1 cup thawed frozen whipped topping
3 tablespoons beer
2 teaspoons lemon juice
1 teaspoon curry powder

1. Blend all ingredients. Chill.
2. Serve with **chilled cooked shrimp.**

About 2 cups

Beer Dessert Sauce

¾ cup sugar
2 tablespoons cornstarch
¼ teaspoon nutmeg
¾ cup water
¾ cup beer
1 egg yolk
2 tablespoons butter or margarine

1. In a heavy saucepan, mix sugar, cornstarch, and nutmeg. Add water and beer gradually, stirring constantly.
2. Cook, stirring constantly, until thickened and clear.
3. Stir a little hot mixture into egg yolk; add to saucepan. Cook slowly, stirring constantly, just until thickened. Do not boil. Stir in butter until melted.
4. Serve warm or cold over cake, gingerbread, or steamed pudding.

About 1¾ cups

Dark Caramel Beer Sauce

Serve this dessert sauce warm on unfrosted cake, steamed pudding, custard, or ice cream.

½ cup packed brown sugar
1½ tablespoons cornstarch
1 can or bottle (12 ounces) beer
2 tablespoons butter or margarine
½ teaspoon vanilla extract

1. In a saucepan, mix brown sugar and cornstarch.
2. Stir in beer. Cook, stirring constantly, until thickened and bubbly.
3. Add butter and vanilla extract. Stir until melted. Serve warm.

About 1⅓ cups

Pilgrim Syrup

This is an old-time syrup dating back to colonial American days. It's delicious on pancakes, waffles, or fritters.

3 cups packed brown sugar
1 can or bottle (12 ounces) beer

Combine ingredients in a saucepan. Heat to boiling; boil about 2 minutes.

About 2 cups

VEGETABLES and SALADS

Vegetables and salads flavored with beer might at first glance seem an unlikely combination. But wait until you try a refreshing molded gelatin salad with an underlying beer flavor, green beans in a beer sauce, fried onion rings in beer batter, or beer-flavored hash brown potatoes. What treats to the taste buds! And so are the other recipes in this chapter. Also turn to the sauces and dressings chapter for some unusual salad dressings. Some of the sauces are delicious on vegetables, too.

German-Style Green Beans

A savory hot bacon sauce flavored with beer is poured over green beans with palate-pleasing results. Serve with an unsauced main dish.

2 packages (9 ounces each) frozen green beans
4 slices bacon, cut in ½-inch pieces
⅓ cup finely chopped onion
¼ to ½ cup beer
2 tablespoons sugar
¼ teaspoon salt
Dash pepper

1. Cook beans according to package directions.
2. Meanwhile, fry bacon in a skillet until lightly browned. Add onion, beer, sugar, salt, and pepper. Heat to boiling.
3. Drain beans, pour beer mixture over, and toss lightly.

6 to 8 servings

Beets Piquant

¼ cup sugar
1 tablespoon cornstarch
1 teaspoon salt
½ teaspoon caraway seed
6 to 8 whole cloves
¼ cup water
1 cup beer
1 can (16 ounces) sliced beets, drained

1. In a medium saucepan, combine sugar, cornstarch, salt, caraway seed, and cloves.
2. Gradually add water and beer while stirring. Cook, stirring constantly, until thickened.
3. Add beets; heat through.

4 servings

Brussels Sprouts and Grapes

1½ pounds fresh Brussels sprouts, cut in half
1 can or bottle (12 ounces) beer
2 teaspoons butter, melted
¼ teaspoon salt
⅛ teaspoon freshly ground white pepper
1 cup seedless white grapes
Snipped parsley

1. Simmer Brussels sprouts in beer in a covered saucepan until tender (about 8 minutes); drain.
2. Drizzle butter over sprouts; sprinkle with salt and pepper. Add grapes; heat thoroughly. Sprinkle with parsley.

6 servings

Red Cabbage, Danish Style

⅓ cup butter or margarine
1 head red cabbage (2 pounds),
    coarsely shredded
1 can or bottle (12 ounces) beer
⅔ cup red currant jelly
½ teaspoon salt

1. Melt butter in a large, heavy saucepan. Add cabbage; cook about 5 minutes to soften, turning frequently.
2. Stir in beer, jelly, and salt. Cover and simmer about 1½ hours, removing cover during last 30 minutes to evaporate most of liquid; stir occasionally.

10 servings, ½ cup each

French-Fried Onion Rings in Beer Batter

These light, crisp onion rings have a batter featuring a hint of beer flavor. The batter may also be used for fresh mushrooms.

1¼ cups flour
1 teaspoon baking powder
1 teaspoon salt
2 tablespoons shortening
1 egg, beaten
1 cup beer
1 large sweet Spanish onion
    Oil for deep frying

1. Mix flour, baking powder, and salt in a bowl. Cut in shortening until mixture resembles fine crumbs.
2. Add egg and beer; beat until smooth.
3. Cut onion into ¼-inch-thick slices; separate into rings.
4. Using a fork, immerse a few onion rings at a time in the batter. Lift out; allow excess batter to drip off. Drop into hot oil (375°F). Fry until golden brown, turning once. Drain on paper towels. Serve hot.

50 to 60 rings; 6 to 8 servings

Hash Brown Potatoes

The potatoes absorb beer while boiling, giving the dish an unusual flavor.

6 medium boiling potatoes (2
    pounds), pared and cubed
1 can or bottle (12 ounces) beer
⅓ cup chopped onion
⅓ cup chopped green pepper
¼ cup butter or margarine
½ teaspoon salt
    Dash pepper

1. In a covered saucepan, boil potatoes in beer until just tender, but not mushy. Remove potatoes with a slotted spoon; chop finely.
2. Add onion and green pepper to saucepan. Add water, if needed, to just cover. Simmer, uncovered, about 5 minutes, or until tender. Drain. Mix with potatoes, salt, and pepper.
3. In a skillet, heat butter until very hot and beginning to brown. Add potato mixture. Cook over medium high heat, turning occasionally, until browned.

6 servings

Beer Pilaff

Substitute beer for water when cooking rice, and the rice takes on an intriguing flavor.

1 medium onion, chopped
2 tablespoons butter or margarine
1 chicken bouillon cube, or 1
    teaspoon chicken stock base
¼ teaspoon salt
    Dash pepper
¾ cup uncooked rice (not instant)
1 can or bottle (12 ounces) beer

1. Sauté onion in butter until soft.
2. Add bouillon, salt, and pepper; stir. Add rice. Cook and stir 1 minute.
3. Add beer. (If package directions specify more than 1½ cups liquid for ¾ cup uncooked rice, use water to make up the difference.)
4. Heat to boiling. Cover, reduce heat, and simmer for 15 minutes, or until tender.

2¾ cups; 4 or 5 servings

Glazed Sweet Potatoes

A sweet beer glaze zips up this healthful vegetable.

⅔ cup packed brown sugar
½ cup beer
¼ cup chopped walnuts
1 tablespoon orange juice
2 teaspoons cornstarch
½ teaspoon grated orange peel
¼ teaspoon salt
1 can (22 ounces) sweet potatoes or yams, drained

1. In a saucepan, combine all ingredients except sweet potatoes. Cook, stirring constantly, until thickened and bubbly.
2. Cut sweet potatoes in chunks; add to glaze. Stir gently until heated through and lightly glazed.

4 to 6 servings

Lagered Sauerkraut with Apples

Serve this German dish with sausage, roast pork, pork chops, or braised beef.

1 can (16 ounces) sauerkraut
1 medium apple
¾ cup beer
1 tablespoon sugar
1 tablespoon butter
½ teaspoon caraway seed
Dash pepper

1. Rinse sauerkraut in a large strainer; drain. Slice apple but do not peel.
2. Place all ingredients in a saucepan. Simmer, uncovered, for about 30 minutes, stirring occasionally, until most of liquid has evaporated and apples are tender.

4 servings

Refreshing Salad Mold

A nice accompaniment to a savory meat dish, especially on warm days.

1 can or bottle (12 ounces) beer
2½ cups ginger ale
2 envelopes unflavored gelatin
2 medium grapefruit, peeled and sectioned

1. Sprinkle gelatin over beer in a saucepan; let stand to soften. Stir over low heat until gelatin is dissolved. Add ginger ale.
2. Chill until partially thickened. Fold in grapefruit sections.
3. Turn into a lightly oiled 5-cup mold. Chill until set. Unmold onto a platter before serving.

8 servings

Piquant Perfection Salad

1½ cups boiling water
1 package (6 ounces) lemon-flavored gelatin
1 can (8 ounces) crushed pineapple in juice
Water
1 can or bottle (12 ounces) beer
3 medium carrots, shredded (about 1½ cups)
½ small head cabbage, finely shredded (about 3 cups)

1. Pour boiling water over gelatin; stir until dissolved.
2. Drain pineapple, thoroughly pressing out and reserving juice. Add enough water to juice to measure ¾ cup.
3. Add juice and beer to gelatin. Chill until partially thickened.
4. Stir in carrots, cabbage, and pineapple. Turn into a shallow pan or oiled 6½-cup ring mold or any 1½-quart mold. Chill until set.
5. Dip mold briefly in hot water; invert on a serving platter.
6. Serve with a dressing of **1 cup mayonnaise** blended with **2 tablespoons beer.**

12 half-cup servings

Beermato Aspic

A refreshing complement to many meat, poultry, and fish dishes.

1 can (18 ounces) tomato juice (2¼ cups)
1 can or bottle (12 ounces) beer
⅓ cup chopped onion
⅓ cup chopped celery leaves (optional)
2½ tablespoons sugar
1 tablespoon lemon juice
½ teaspoon salt
1 bay leaf
2 envelopes unflavored gelatin
¼ cup cold water

1. Combine tomato juice (reserve ¼ cup), beer, onion, celery leaves, sugar, lemon juice, salt, and bay leaf in a saucepan. Simmer, uncovered, 10 minutes.
2. Meanwhile, sprinkle gelatin over cold water and reserved tomato juice in a large bowl; let stand to soften.
3. Strain hot tomato juice mixture into bowl; stir until gelatin is completely dissolved.
4. Pour into a lightly oiled 1-quart mold. Chill until firm. Unmold onto crisp **salad greens.**

8 servings

Note: For individual aspics, turn mixture into 8 oiled ½-cup molds. Chill until firm.

Beer-Curried Fruit

An unusual accompaniment for baked ham, pork, poultry, or lamb. A nice winter brunch dish, too. It's pretty on a buffet table.

½ cup packed brown sugar
1 tablespoon cornstarch
2 to 3 teaspoons curry powder
¾ cup beer
¼ cup butter or margarine
1 tablespoon grated orange peel
1 can (30 ounces) cling peach slices, drained
1 can (29 ounces) pear halves or slices, drained
2 cans (11 ounces each) mandarin oranges, drained
2 bananas, thinly sliced

1. In a large saucepan, combine sugar, cornstarch, and curry powder. Stir in beer. Cook, stirring constantly, until thickened and clear.
2. Add butter and orange peel; stir until melted.
3. Add peaches, pears, and mandarin oranges. (If using pear halves, cut into slices.) Cover and simmer about 10 minutes. Stir in bananas.
4. Turn into a serving dish, chafing dish, or warming dish. Sprinkle with **flaked coconut.**

7 cups

Tangy Cabbage Mold

A cool, tart taste that is nice with a hearty main dish. If you wish, serve with mayonnaise.

1 **envelope unflavored gelatin**	1. Soften gelatin in cold water in a saucepan. Stir over low heat until dissolved.
¼ **cup cold water**	
¼ **cup sugar**	2. Add sugar, lemon juice, and salt; stir until dissolved. Add beer. Chill until partially thickened.
2 **tablespoons lemon juice**	
½ **teaspoon salt**	3. Stir in cabbage and green pepper.
1 **can or bottle (12 ounces) beer**	4. Turn into a 3½-cup mold, a shallow 1½-quart oblong casserole (8x6 inches), or 6 individual molds.
1½ **cups shredded cabbage (about ¼ of a 2-pound head)**	
½ **green pepper, shredded**	

6 servings

Hot Potato Salad

Bacon and beer flavor the slightly sweet sauce on these German-style potatoes. Serve with hot dogs, bratwurst, or Polish sausage. Beer is the perfect beverage.

6 **medium boiling potatoes (2 pounds)**	1. Place unpeeled potatoes in a large saucepan; add water to cover. Heat to boiling. Boil, uncovered, for 20 minutes, or until tender. Peel and cube; turn into a serving dish.
10 **slices bacon (½ pound)**	
½ **cup chopped onion**	2. Meanwhile, cook bacon until crisp; leave drippings in skillet. Crumble bacon over potatoes.
½ **cup beer**	
1 to 1½ **tablespoons sugar**	3. Add onion to skillet. Sauté until tender. Add beer, sugar, salt, and celery seed. Heat to boiling, stirring occasionally. Pour over potatoes; toss lightly.
1 to 1½ **teaspoons salt**	
1 **teaspoon celery seed**	

6 servings

DESSERTS

Yes, beer can star even in the last course of a meal, and the results are surprisingly excellent! The other ingredients—sugar, spices, eggs, fruits, and so forth—seem to transform and blend the original bitter beer flavor into a sweet, mellow, palate-pleasing whole. With cakes, beer does something different. The beer flavor is almost gone, but lightness and extra tenderness are given to the end product.

Beer dessert possibilities are numerous. Included here are about two dozen ideas for pies, cakes, fillings, frostings, puddings, fruit desserts, and even a beer ice. Some are family desserts; others are elegant company meal finales. Beer desserts in the menu section include Holiday Fruitcake, Beer Balls, Scandinavian Fruit Soup, and Gingerbread Pear Upside-down Cake.

Lemon-Beer Sponge Pie

This pie bakes with a puddinglike layer on the bottom, a cakelike layer on the top. The beer flavor is subtle.

1 unbaked 9-inch pie shell
4 eggs, separated
¾ cup sugar
¼ cup flour
3 tablespoons butter or margarine, softened
2 teaspoons grated lemon peel
1 can or bottle (12 ounces) beer
2 tablespoons lemon juice

1. Bake pie shell at 450°F 10 minutes.
2. Beat egg whites until foamy. Gradually add half of sugar, continuing beating until stiff peaks form.
3. In a separate bowl, beat remaining sugar, flour, butter, peel and egg yolks. Mix in beer and lemon juice.
4. Fold beaten egg whites into yolk mixture. Turn into partially baked pie shell.
5. Bake at 350°F about 50 minutes, or until set. Cool to room temperature before slicing.

One 9-inch pie

Peanuts-and-Beer Pie

Peanuts and beer are frequent partners—for snacking, at the ball park, at parties. So what a natural idea it would be to combine peanuts and beer in a sweet dessert pie. It's a memorable combination. This is a chiffon-type pie made fluffy with beaten egg whites and firmed with gelatin. It goes into a prebaked shell.

Pastry for 9-inch pie shell
1 can or bottle (12 ounces) beer
1 envelope unflavored gelatin
½ cup packed brown sugar
3 eggs, separated
1 teaspoon vanilla extract
6 ounces salted peanuts (1¼ cups), chopped
¼ cup granulated sugar

1. Roll out pastry and fit into pie plate. Do not cut off excess pastry, but fold under and make high fluted sides. Prick bottom and sides thoroughly with fork.
2. Bake at 450°F 15 minutes, until light golden brown. Cool.
3. Pour beer into top of a double boiler; sprinkle with gelatin. Add brown sugar and slightly beaten egg yolks.
4. Cook over boiling water, stirring constantly, until slightly thickened and gelatin is dissolved (8 to 10 minutes). Add vanilla extract.
5. Chill until partially thickened. Stir in peanuts.
6. Beat egg whites until foamy. Gradually add granulated sugar, continuing beating until stiff peaks form. Fold in peanut-gelatin mixture. Turn into baked shell. Chill.

One 9-inch pie

Brewmaster's Poppyseed Cake

A scrumptious, moist, and tender cake that everyone will rave about. It needs no frosting.

Cake:
- 1 package (2-layer size) regular yellow cake mix
- 1 small package instant vanilla pudding and pie filling
- 4 eggs
- 1 cup beer
- ½ cup oil
- ¼ cup poppyseed

Glaze:
- ½ cup sugar
- ½ cup beer
- ¼ cup butter

1. Place cake mix, dry pudding, eggs, beer, oil, and poppyseed in an electric mixer bowl. Blend on low speed. Then beat on medium speed for 2 minutes.
2. Turn into a well-greased and floured 10-inch Bundt or tube pan.
3. Bake at 350°F 50 to 55 minutes, or until done.
4. Cool in pan 15 minutes. Turn out on rack.
5. To prepare glaze, boil ingredients for 5 minutes. Prick warm cake with skewer in many places. Brush warm glaze generously over top and sides. Cool. (If desired, sift confectioners' sugar over top; cake needs no frosting.)

1 large cake; 16 servings

Velvety Chocolate Cake

This excellent chocolate cake has an extremely moist and tender crumb.

- 2¾ cups sifted cake flour
- 2 teaspoons baking powder
- 1 teaspoon baking soda
- ¼ teaspoon salt
- ¾ cup butter or margarine
- 1 cup packed brown sugar
- ⅔ cup granulated sugar
- 3 eggs
- 3 ounces (3 squares) unsweetened chocolate, melted and cooled
- 1 can or bottle (12 ounces) beer

1. Sift dry ingredients together.
2. Cream butter and sugars until very light and fluffy.
3. Add eggs, one at a time, beating thoroughly at medium speed of electric mixer. Beat in chocolate.
4. Add sifted dry ingredients alternately with beer, beating at low speed until blended after each addition.
5. Turn into 2 greased and waxed-paper-lined 9-inch round layer cake pans.
6. Bake at 350°F 35 minutes, or until done. Cool in pans 10 minutes; turn out on wire racks. When cool, frost with Cocoa-Beer Icing (page 88) or any favorite icing.

One 2-layer 9-inch cake

Nutmeg Cake

A moist, flavorful cake with a very tender crumb. Fill it with Lemon-Beer Filling or Orange-Beer Filling. Frost with any white frosting.

- 3 cups sifted cake flour
- 1 tablespoon baking powder
- 2 teaspoons nutmeg
- ½ teaspoon salt
- ¾ cup butter or margarine
- 2 teaspoons vanilla extract
- 1 cup granulated sugar
- ¾ cup packed brown sugar
- 2 whole eggs
- 2 egg whites
- 1 can or bottle (12 ounces) beer
  Lemon-Beer or Orange-Beer Filling (page 87)
  White frosting, any type

1. Sift dry ingredients together.
2. Cream butter with vanilla extract and sugars until light and fluffy. Add eggs and whites, one at a time, beating well after each addition (medium speed of mixer).
3. Alternately add sifted dry ingredients in thirds and beer in halves to creamed mixture, beating on low speed just until smooth after each addition.
4. Turn into 2 greased and waxed-paper-lined 9-inch round layer cake pans.
5. Bake at 350°F 30 to 35 minutes, or until cake tests done. Cool in pans about 10 minutes. Turn out onto wire racks. Cool completely before filling and frosting.

One 2-layer 9-inch cake

Note: If not making a filling requiring egg yolks, use 3 whole eggs in batter.

Raisin-Nut Spice Cake

Serve this moist, dark, and delectable cake any time of year with whipped cream, ice cream, or Beer Dessert Sauce on top. It is delicious served warm with hard sauce during the holiday season.

> 3 cups sifted cake flour
> 2 teaspoons baking powder
> 1 teaspoon baking soda
> ½ teaspoon cinnamon
> ½ teaspoon nutmeg
> ¼ teaspoon ginger
> ¼ teaspoon salt
> 1 can or bottle (12 ounces) beer
> 1 cup raisins (5 ounces)
> ¾ cup butter or margarine
> 1 cup sugar
> ½ cup molasses
> 2 eggs
> ¾ cup chopped nuts (3 ounces)
>   Glaze

1. Sift dry ingredients together. Set aside.
2. Heat beer and raisins to simmering; let stand about 15 minutes to plump.
3. Cream butter and sugar until light and fluffy; add molasses.
4. Add eggs, one at a time, beating well after each addition.
5. Add dry ingredients alternately in thirds with beer drained from raisins, beating just until well blended. Stir in raisins and nuts.
6. Turn into a well-greased and floured 10-inch Bundt pan or angel food cake pan (nonstick pan preferred).
7. Bake at 350°F 1 hour, or until done.
8. Let stand in pan about 10 minutes; invert onto cake rack. Cool. Cover with foil or store in airtight container. Cake slices better if made a day in advance.
9. Prepare a glaze by thinning **1 cup sifted confectioners' sugar** with **beer** or **milk.** Drizzle over cake shortly before serving.

1 large cake; 16 servings

Old English Cheesecake

Raisins, almonds, lemon peel, and beer delectably perk up the flavor of this rich dessert.

Crust:
> 1¼ cups all-purpose flour
> ¼ cup sugar
> ⅓ cup butter or margarine
> 4 tablespoons cold beer

Filling:
> ½ cup golden raisins (2½ ounces), chopped
> ⅓ cup almonds (2 ounces), finely chopped
> 1 tablespoon grated lemon peel
> 1 pound cottage cheese
> ½ cup flour
> 4 eggs
> 1 cup sugar
> ¾ cup beer
> ⅛ teaspoon nutmeg

1. For crust, mix flour and sugar; cut in butter until crumbly. Add beer 1 tablespoon at a time, stirring with a fork. Shape dough into a ball. Chill.
2. Roll out on floured surface to a 13- to 14-inch circle. Fold in quarters. Gently unfold in a 9-inch springform pan. Even edge of crust so it extends about 2 inches up sides of pan (1½ inches up sides if using a 10-inch pan). Prick all over with fork.
3. Bake at 425°F 10 minutes. Prick again and press to sides. Bake 10 minutes more, or until slightly golden.
4. For filling, mix chopped raisins, almonds, and peel.
5. Process cottage cheese, flour, and eggs until smooth, using food processor or electric blender. (Do in several batches in blender.)
6. Add sugar, beer, and nutmeg; blend until smooth. Stir in raisin mixture. Pour into cooled shell.
7. Bake at 300°F 1¼ to 1½ hours, or until set. Cool to room temperature for serving. Dust with **confectioners' sugar** and top with **whole unblanched almonds.**

8 to 10 servings

Easy Walnut Cake

When filled with Orange-Beer Filling or Lemon-Beer Filling, this cake doesn't even need an icing—but add one of your choice, if you wish. Otherwise, sift confectioners' sugar over the top.

1 package (2-layer size) yellow
   cake mix
Beer
Water
2 eggs
⅔ cup finely chopped walnuts
Orange-Beer Filling or
   Lemon-Beer Filling

1. Mix cake batter according to package directions. Use the exact amount of liquid called for, but substitute beer for all or part of the water. (If making Orange-Beer Filling, set aside ½ cup beer from a can for filling and use 1 cup in cake. For Lemon-Beer Filling, set aside ¾ cup beer for filling and use ¾ cup in cake. If not making beer-flavored filling, substitute beer for all of the water in cake.)
2. Blend in walnuts.
3. Turn batter into 2 greased and waxed-paper-lined 9-inch round layer cake pans.
4. Bake at 350°F 30 minutes, or until a wooden pick inserted in center comes out clean. Cool in pans 10 minutes; turn out onto wire racks. Cool completely before filling and frosting.

One 2-layer 9-inch cake

Orange-Beer Filling

⅓ cup sugar
1½ tablespoons cornstarch
⅛ teaspoon salt
½ cup beer
⅓ cup orange juice
1 egg yolk
2 teaspoons grated orange peel
2 teaspoons butter or margarine

1. In top of a double boiler, combine sugar, cornstarch, and salt. Stir in beer and orange juice. Cook over direct heat, stirring constantly, until thickened and clear.
2. Add a little hot mixture to egg yolk; return to double-boiler top. Cook over hot water, stirring constantly, 4 to 5 minutes.
3. Stir in peel and butter. Cool before spreading on cake.

About 1 cup; enough to fill two 8- or 9-inch layers

Lemon-Beer Filling

A tart filling to spread between two layers of an 8- or 9-inch cake.

½ cup sugar
2 tablespoons cornstarch
⅛ teaspoon salt
¾ cup beer
2 teaspoons grated lemon peel
2 tablespoons lemon juice
2 egg yolks

1. In top of a double boiler, combine sugar, cornstarch, and salt. Stir in beer. Cook over direct heat, stirring constantly, until thickened and clear.
2. Stir in lemon peel and juice.
3. Add a little hot mixture to egg yolks; return to double boiler top. Cook over hot water, stirring constantly, for 4 to 5 minutes. Cool before spreading on cake.

About 1 cup

White Beer Icing

3 tablespoons butter
3 cups sifted confectioners' sugar
3 to 4 tablespoons beer

1. Cream butter.
2. Add confectioners' sugar alternately with beer, until frosting is fluffy and of spreading consistency.

1⅔ cups; for tops and sides of 2 round 8- or 9-inch layers

Cocoa-Beer Icing

A light chocolate icing with a very mild beer flavor.

¼ pound butter or margarine,
   softened
3½ cups sifted confectioners' sugar
⅓ cup cocoa
⅛ teaspoon salt
⅓ cup beer (about)

1. Cream butter with part of confectioners' sugar.
2. Add cocoa, salt, and a little beer. Beat until smooth.
3. Add remaining sugar alternately with enough beer to make icing of spreading consistency, beating until fluffy.

2 cups; for tops and sides of two 9-inch layers

Spicy Fruit Gelatin "with a Head"

Serve this fruited gelatin dessert in pilsner glasses, if you have them, and top with whipped cream or whipped topping to simulate the foam on beer.

1 can or bottle (12 ounces) beer
2 tablespoons packed brown
   sugar
1 stick cinnamon
4 whole cloves
1 package (3 ounces)
   orange-flavored gelatin
1 can (8¼ ounces) crushed
   pineapple
   Water

1. Place beer, brown sugar, cinnamon, and cloves in a saucepan. Heat to boiling. Add gelatin; stir until dissolved.
2. Let stand at room temperature until lukewarm to mellow flavors. Remove spices.
3. Drain pineapple thoroughly, reserving liquid. Add water to liquid to measure ½ cup. Stir into gelatin mixture. Chill until partially thickened.
4. Fold in pineapple. Spoon into pilsner or parfait glasses. Chill until firm.
5. To serve, top with a "head" of whipped cream or prepared whipped topping.

4 or 5 servings

Zesty Beer Ice

You've heard of champagne sherbet, so why not a beer ice? Those who try it are in for a delicious surprise. It's especially nice on hot days or following a heavy meal. Lemon gives a zest to the taste.

1 envelope unflavored gelatin
2 cans or bottles (12 ounces each)
   beer
1 cup sugar
2 teaspoons grated lemon peel
½ cup lemon juice

1. Sprinkle gelatin over 1 can beer in a saucepan. Let stand 5 minutes to soften.
2. Add sugar. Cook over low heat just until dissolved.
3. Add remaining 1 can beer, lemon peel, and juice. Turn into a shallow pan.
4. Freeze until firm, stirring several times. Pack into a 1-quart covered container.

1 quart

Baked Stuffed Apples

6 medium cooking apples (about
   2 pounds)
½ cup raisins
½ cup packed brown sugar
1 teaspoon cinnamon
1 cup beer

1. Core apples. Remove 1-inch strip of peel around top.
2. Mix raisins, brown sugar, and cinnamon. Fill apple centers.
3. Place apples in a baking dish. Pour beer over.
4. Bake at 350°F 40 to 45 minutes, or until tender, basting occasionally.
5. Cool to room temperature, basting while cooling. Serve with its own sauce. If desired, add cream or Beer Dessert Sauce (page 76).

6 servings

Beer Bread Pudding

1½ cups milk
1 can or bottle (12 ounces) beer
3 eggs
½ cup packed brown sugar
½ teaspoon vanilla extract
¼ teaspoon cinnamon
¼ teaspoon nutmeg
¼ teaspoon salt
4 cups dry bread cubes (6 slices)

1. Scald milk and beer.
2. Beat eggs with brown sugar, vanilla extract, cinnamon, nutmeg, and salt. Add scalded milk and beer gradually while stirring. Add bread.
3. Turn into a greased 1½- or 2-quart casserole. Set in a pan of boiling water.
4. Bake at 325°F 50 minutes, or until a knife inserted in center comes out clean. Serve hot or cold.

6 servings

Raisin-Beer Pudding

Try putting beer in a simple pudding. You'll discover a surprisingly delicious and unusual flavor treat.

2 eggs
1½ cups milk
½ cup sugar
¼ cup quick-cooking tapioca
¼ teaspoon nutmeg
⅛ teaspoon salt
1 can or bottle (12 ounces) beer
½ cup raisins

1. In a heavy 2-quart saucepan, beat eggs. Add milk, sugar, tapioca, nutmeg, and salt. Let stand 5 minutes.
2. Cook, stirring constantly, to simmering. Add beer gradually while stirring; add raisins. Cook and stir just to boiling.
3. Pour into dessert dishes.

About 1 quart; 6 to 8 servings

Spicy Butterscotch Pudding

This pudding may also be put in 4 to 6 baked tart shells or an 8-inch baked pie shell.

1 package (4-serving size) butterscotch pudding and pie filling (not instant)
⅔ cup instant nonfat dry milk
1 teaspoon pumpkin pie spice
1 cup beer
1 cup water
Whipped cream or thawed frozen whipped dessert topping

1. In a heavy saucepan, combine pudding mix, dry milk, and spice. Stir in beer and water.
2. Cook over medium heat, stirring constantly, until mixture boils.
3. Pour into 4 pudding dishes. Cover surfaces with plastic wrap. Chill until set. Serve topped with whipped cream or dessert topping.

4 servings

Chocolate-Beer Pudding Cake

A fun dessert to make and bake. A hot chocolate-beer syrup is poured over cake batter in the pan. After baking, a puddinglike layer forms in the bottom. The cake is then inverted.

Batter:
- 1½ cups all-purpose flour
- ¾ cup sugar
- 1 tablespoon unsweetened cocoa
- 1½ teaspoons baking powder
- ½ teaspoon baking soda
- ¼ teaspoon salt
- ¾ cup beer
- ⅓ cup oil
- 1 egg, slightly beaten

Syrup:
- 1 tablespoon unsweetened cocoa
- ¾ cup beer
- ⅓ cup packed brown sugar
- ⅓ cup granulated sugar

1. For batter, mix dry ingredients; make a well in center. Add beer, oil, and egg. Beat just until smooth.
2. For syrup, make a paste of cocoa and a little beer. Add remaining beer and sugars. Heat to boiling.
3. Pour batter into a greased 8-inch square baking pan. Drizzle syrup over top.
4. Bake at 350°F 40 minutes.
5. Cool about 5 minutes. Loosen sides of cake from pan; invert onto platter. Even out pudding layer with knife. Serve warm or cool.

6 to 8 servings

Currant-Apple Fritters

Serve as a hot dessert sprinkled with confectioners' sugar. Or top with syrup and serve for breakfast.

- 1 cup all-purpose flour
- 1½ teaspoons baking powder
- ¼ teaspoon cinnamon
- ¼ teaspoon salt
- ½ cup beer
- ½ cup currants
- ½ cup chopped pared apple
- 2 eggs, slightly beaten
- 1 teaspoon oil
- Fat for deep frying
- Confectioners' sugar

1. Combine flour, baking powder, cinnamon, and salt. Add beer, currants, apple, eggs, and oil. Stir to blend well.
2. Drop by rounded teaspoonfuls into hot deep fat heated to 365°F. Fry until browned. Drain on paper towels.
3. Keep hot in oven until serving time. While still hot, roll in confectioners' sugar.

About 30 fritters; 6 to 8 servings

Peach Cobbler

- 1 can (29 ounces) sliced peaches
- 2 teaspoons lemon juice
- ¼ teaspoon cinnamon
- 1½ tablespoons cornstarch
- ¾ cup beer
- 1 cup all-purpose flour
- 1½ teaspoons baking powder
- ¼ teaspoon salt
- 3 tablespoons shortening

1. Drain peaches, reserving syrup.
2. Lightly toss together peaches, lemon juice, and cinnamon. Arrange in a buttered shallow 1½-quart baking dish, 10 x 6 inches, or 8 inches square.
3. In a small saucepan, blend cornstarch, ¼ cup reserved syrup, and ¾ cup beer. Cook, stirring constantly, until thickened and clear. Pour over peaches.
4. Bake at 400°F 10 to 15 minutes, or until bubbly.
5. Meanwhile, mix flour, baking powder, and salt. Add ½ cup more reserved syrup (or use ½ cup beer plus 1 tablespoon sugar). Stir just until dough forms a ball.
6. Drop by large spoonfuls onto peaches. Continue baking 25 minutes.

8 servings

BEVERAGES

Cooking With Beer

BEER
BEER
BEER

As pleasurable as beer is to drink the way it comes from the brewmaster, beer can also be combined with other ingredients for tantalizing drinks and punches. Some are designed to be served hot, others cold. Several are centuries-old drinks dating back to early English alehouses, other European countries, or American colonial times. The famous Old English Hot Wassail appears in the menu section as a holiday open-house warmer. Another old drink, Hot Spiced Beer and Rum, is suggested for the winter chili supper. Try a variety of these unusual beer beverages as a treat for your friends.

American Colonial Flip

A flip was among the most popular drinks in early American taverns. It was made frothy by beating the eggs, then pouring the beer and eggs back and forth in two large pitchers. The drink was also served hot by thrusting a red-hot iron poker or loggerhead into the drink. It was served in large drinking vessels, each man consuming several quarts. More moderate portions are suggested for today.

> 2 cans or bottles (12 ounces each) beer
> ½ cup gin, rum, or brandy
> 3 eggs
> ¼ cup sugar
> Grated nutmeg

1. Heat beer and gin, if desired, but do not boil. Pour into a large pitcher.
2. Beat eggs with sugar until thick; pour into a second pitcher. Gradually add beer mixture to eggs, stirring constantly.
3. Froth by carefully and quickly pouring back and forth between the two pitchers. Pour into mugs.

3 or 4 servings

Old-fashioned Posset

This hot drink from old England was also consumed during the American colonial era. It was the drink to have when one felt tired or had a cold; it also become a Christmas Eve custom. There are several variations.

> 1½ cups milk
> ¼ cup sugar
> ¼ teaspoon cinnamon
> 1 can or bottle (12 ounces) ale or beer
> 2 to 3 toast squares or stars

1. Heat milk with sugar and cinnamon until sugar is dissolved.
2. Add ale; heat but do not simmer or boil.
3. Pour into 2 or 3 mugs. Float toast on top. If desired, increase recipe and serve from punch bowl.

2 or 3 servings

Holiday Eggnog

This homemade eggnog is rich, yet is not heavily alcoholic. If you've never considered beer in eggnog, you'll be quite pleasantly surprised at the delectable flavor.

> 3 eggs, separated
> ½ cup sugar
> 2 cups milk
> 1 can or bottle (12 ounces) beer
> ¼ cup brandy or bourbon
> 1 cup whipping cream, whipped
> Nutmeg

1. Beat egg yolks with ¼ cup sugar until very thick. Gradually stir in milk, beer, and brandy.
2. Beat egg whites until foamy. Gradually beat in ¼ cup sugar, continuing beating until stiff peaks form.
3 Fold whites into yolk-beer mixture. Chill.
4. Just before serving, fold in whipped cream. Serve in small punch cups; sprinkle with nutmeg.

6 cups; 12 half-cup servings

Belgian Hot Beer and Wine

1 can or bottle (12 ounces)
1½ cups white wine
⅓ cup sugar
1 cinnamon stick
 Peel of ½ lemon, cut in strips
1 tablespoon cornstarch
½ cup warm milk
2 egg yolks

1. Heat beer, wine, sugar, cinnamon, and lemon peel for 10 to 15 minutes; do not simmer or boil.
2. In a heavy saucepan, mix cornstarch and milk; beat in egg yolks. Cook slowly, stirring constantly, until thickened.
3. Stir hot beer into egg mixture. Serve immediately in small punch cups.

3 cups; 6 servings

Beer Nog

3 eggs
1 can or bottle (12 ounces) beer
1½ cups milk
⅓ cup sugar
⅛ teaspoon nutmeg

Beat eggs until frothy. Add remaining ingredients. Serve cold; or heat slightly for serving warm; do not simmer or boil. Sprinkle with nutmeg.

Beer Bloody Mary

1 can or bottle (12 ounces) beer
1 can (12 ounces) tomato juice
 Dash Worcestershire sauce
 Dash Tabasco

Combine ingredients; pour over ice in old-fashioned glasses.

3 or 4 servings

Cold Beer Punch

3 bottles or cans (12 ounces each) beer, chilled
¼ cup sherry
¼ cup brandy
¼ cup bar sugar or confectioners' sugar
3 tablespoons lemon juice
 Few pieces lemon peel
 Dash nutmeg

Mix all ingredients in a pitcher. Pour over ice in low glasses or punch cups. Sprinkle with nutmeg.

5 cups

Shandy Tang

½ cup beer or ale
½ cup lemon-lime soda
 Ice cubes

Pour beer and soda over ice cubes in a tall glass. Stir lightly. May also be served without ice; have ingredients well chilled.

1 serving

Black Velvet

Guinness stout, chilled
Champagne, chilled

Fill an 8-ounce highball glass half full with stout and half with champagne. Pour gently so it doesn't overflow. Proportion of stout may be decreased.

1 serving

INDEX

Alaus su Agunom Sriuba   45
Appetizers
   Appetizer Puffs   34
   Chili Nuts   36
   Cocktail Party Sausages   36
   German Beer Cheese   36
   Marinated Mushrooms   35
   Pickled Shrimp   34
   Shamrock Canapés   20
   Shrimp Dunk   35
   Shrimp Spread   35
   Tangy Cheese Dip   36
Apple Fritters, Currant-   90
Apples, Baked Stuffed   88
Apples, Lagered
   Sauerkraut with   80
Aspic, Beermato   81

Balls, Beer   32
Batter for Fritters, Beer   42
Bean Salad, Marinated   27
Beans, German Style Green   78
Beans 'n' Beer Bake   22
Beef
   Applesauce-Topped, and
     Sausage Loaf   61
   Bachelor's Steak   58
   Brewerburgers   58
   Caraway Meat Loaf   60
   Chili with Beer   19
   English Meat Patties   58
   Flemish Beef Stew   56
   Hearty Beef-Nooodle Soup   48
   Jiffy Beer Chili   61
   Luxemburg Stew   64
   Munich Beef   56
   Mushroom-Beer Steaks   59
   Old-World Short Ribs   60
   Savory Beef Stew   57
   Scandinavian Sailors'
     Beef Casserole   58
Beer and Rum, Hot Spiced   18
Beer and Wine, Belgian Hot   93
Beets, Piquant   78
Beverages
   American Colonial Flip   92
   Beer Bloody Mary   93
   Beer Nog   93
   Belgian Hot Beer and Wine   93
   Black Velvet   93
   Cold Beer Punch   93
   Holiday Eggnog   92
   Hot Spiced Beer and Rum   18
   Old English Hot Wassail   31
   Old Fashioned Posset   92
   Shandy Tang   93

Bier Fisch   68
Bierkäse   36
Biscuits, Beer-Can   41
Biscuits, Cheese-Beer   41
Black Velvet   93
Bloody Mary, Beer   93
Bratwurst in Beer for a
   Crowd, Backyard   23
Bread
   Beer-Cheese Bread with Raisins 38
   Bock Beer   39
   Irish Soda Bread with Currants   21
   Jiffy Beer   38
   Limpa   17
   Old-Style Cornbread   40
   Peasant Black   39
   Pudding, Beer   89
Brewerburgers   38
Brussels Sprouts and Grapes   78
Buck, Golden   52
Butterscotch Pudding, Spicy   89

Cabbage, Danish Style, Red   79
Cabbage Mold, Tangy   82
Cabbage, Sweet-Sour Red   29
Cake
   Brewermaster's Poppyseed   85
   Chocolate-Beer Pudding   90
   Easy Walnut   87
   Gingerbread Pear
     Upside-down Cake   27
   Nutmeg   85
   Raisin-Nut Spice   86
   Velvety Chocolate   85
Canapés, Shamrock   20
Carbonade à la Flamande   56
Casserole, Bavarian   61
Casserole, Lagered Ham
   and Noodle   62
Casserole, Scandinavian
   Sailors' Beef   58
Cheddar Spritz Sticks   19
Cheese
   Beery Strata   51
   Cheddar-Beer Omelets   51
   Cheddar Spritz Sticks   19
   Dutch Fondue   54
   German Beer Cheese   36
   Soufflé au Bière   51
   Tangy Cheese Dip   36
   Tomato Rabbit   52
   Tuna and Swiss Cheese Pie   70
   Welsh Rabbit   52
Cheesecake, Old English   86
Chicken
   African-Style   67
   and Rice in Beer   67
   Brewers'   66
   Broiled Marinated   67
   Crunchy Fried   68
   Roast, with Orange-Beer Sauce   66
   Spiced Fruited   25

Chili con Cerveza   19
Chili, Jiffy Beer   61
Chili Nuts   36
Chili Sauce, Beer   22
Chili with Beer   19
Chops, German Veal   64
Chops with Beer Gravy,
   Breaded Pork   60
Cobbler, Peach   90
Coffeecake, Streusel   38
Cornbread, Old-Style   40
Corn, Mexican Style,
   Squash and   25
Cream, Molded Spanish   19
Cucumber Salad   17
Cucumber Salad with
   Sour Cream   30

Desserts
   Baked Stuffed Apples   88
   Beer Balls   32
   Beer Bread Pudding   89
   Brewermaster's Poppyseed
     Cake   85
   Chocolate-Beer Pudding
     Cake   90
   Coconut Flan   26
   Currant-Apple Fritters   90
   Easy Walnut Cake   87
   Gingerbread Pear
     Upside-Down Cake   27
   Hazelnut Torte   30
   Holiday Fruitcake   32
   July 4th Fruit Tart   22
   Lemon-Beer Sponge Pie   84
   Molded Spanish Cream   19
   Nutmeg Cake   85
   Old English Cheesecake   86
   Peach Cobbler   90
   Peanuts-and-Beer Pie   84
   Raisin-Beer Pudding   89
   Raisin-Nut Spice Cake   86
   Scandinavian Fruit Soup   18
   Spicy Butterscotch Pudding   89
   Spicy Fruit Gelatin
     "with a Head"   88
   Streusel Coffeecake   38
   Velvety Chocolate Cake   85
   Zesty Beer Ice   88
Dressing
   Beer Oil Salad   74
   Curried   75
   for Cole Slaw, Beer   75
   for Potato Salad, Beer   75
   Ginger-Beer Mayonnaise   75
   Poppyseed-Beer Salad   74
Dumplings, Caraway   29

Eggnog, Holiday   92
Eggs, Alsatian Style   53
Eggs, Savory Baked   52

Filling, Creamy Rum 30
Filling, Lemon-Beer 87
Filling, Orange-Beer 87
Fish
  Beer-Batter Fried Sole 68
  Fillets, Saucy 69
  Flemish Style Mock Lobster 69
  German Beer 68
  Salmon with Sour Cream
    Sauce, Cold 16
  Tuna and Swiss Cheese Pie 70
  Tuna-Macaroni Bake 70
Flan, Coconut 26
Flip, American Colonial 92
Fondue, Dutch 54
Franks and Bean Soup, Easy 46
Fritters, Beer Batter for 42
Fritters, Currant-Apple 90
Fruit, Beer-Curried 81
Fruitcake, Holiday 32
Fruit Gelatin "with a Head",
  Spicy 88
Fruit Soup, Scandinavian 18

Gaufres Bruxelloises 41
Gelatin "with a Head",
  Spicy Fruit 88
Grapes, Brussels Sprouts and 78
Green Beans, German Style 78
Griddlecakes with Pilgrim
  Syrup, Beer 40

Ham and Noodle Casserole,
  Lagered 62
Heisse Biersuppe 28

Ice, Zesty Beer 88
Icing, Cocoa-Beer 88
Icing, White Beer 87

Kabobs, Piquant Lamb 63
Kraut, Sausage-Stuffed
  Rouladen with
  Tomato-Beer 57

Lamb
  Irish Stew with Ale 20
  Orange-Ginger Lamb Chops 62
  Piquant Lamb Kabobs 63
Leek Soup, Farm-Style 47
Lentil Soup, Savory 47
Limpa Bread 17
Lobster, Flemish Style, Mock 69

Mayonnaise, Ginger-Beer 75
Meat
  African-Style Chicken 67
  Applesauce-Topped Beef and
    Sausage Loaf 61
  Bachelor's Steak 58
  Backyard Bratwurst in Beer
    for a Crowd 23

Breaded Pork Chops with Beer
  Gravy 60
Brewerburgers 58
Brewers' Chicken 66
Caraway Meat Loaf 60
Chicken and Rice in Beer 67
Cocktail Party Sausages 36
Crunchy Fried Chicken 68
English Meat Patties 58
Flemish Beef Stew 56
German Pork Roast in Spicy
  Beer Sauce 29
German Veal Chops 64
Irish Stew with Ale 20
Jiffy Beer Chili 61
Lagered Ham and Noodle
  Casserole 62
Luxemburg Stew 64
Marinated Broiled Chicken 67
Marinated Venison in Cream
  Gravy 59
Munich Beef 56
Mushroom-Beer Steaks 59
Old World Short Ribs 60
Orange-Ginger Lamb Chops 62
Piquant Lamb Kabobs 63
Pork and Beans, Mexican Style 24
Roast Chicken with
  Orange-Beer Sauce 66
Sausage in Beer 64
Sausage-Stuffed Rouladen with
  Tomato-Beer Kraut 57
Savory Beef Stew 57
Savory Spareribs 62
Scandinavian Sailors'
  Beef Casserole 58
Scandinavian Style Fruited
  Pork Roast 63
Swedish Meatballs 17
Meatballs, Swedish 17
Meat Loaf, Caraway 60
Meat Patties, English 58
Muffins, Orange 42
Mushroom-Beer Soufflé 53
Mushrooms, Marinated 35

Nog, Beer 93
Nuts, Chili 36

Oeufs à l'Alsace 53
Omelets, Cheddar-Beer 51
Onion Rings in Beer Batter,
  French-Fried 79

Pancakes, Danish 40
Peach Cobbler 90
Pie, Lemon-Beer Sponge 84
Pie, Peanuts-and-Beer 84
Pilaff, Beer 79
Pizza, Beer Drinker's Deep-Pan 50
Pork
  and Beans, Mexican Style 24

Bavarian Casserole 61
Breaded Pork Chops with
  Beer Gravy 60
Fruited Pork Roast,
  Scandinavian Style 63
German Pork Roast in Spicy
  Beer Sauce 29
Lagered Ham and Noodle
  Casserole 62
Savory Spareribs 62
Posset, Old-Fashioned 92
Potatoes, Glazed Sweet 80
Potatoes, Hash Brown 79
Potato Salad, Hot 82
Potato Salad with Tart
  Dressing, Cold 23
Poultry
  African-Style Chicken 67
  Brewers' Chicken 66
  Chicken and Rice in Beer 67
  Crunchy Fried Chicken 68
  Marinated Broiled Chicken 67
  Roast Chicken with
    Orange-Beer Sauce 66
  Spiced Fruited Chicken 25
Pretzels, Soft 42
Pronto Chili con Cerveza 61
Pudding, Beer Bread 89
Pudding Cake, Chocolate-Beer 90
Pudding, Raisin-Beer 89
Pudding, Spicy Butterscotch 89
Punch, Cold Beer 93

Rabbit, Tomato 52
Rabbit, Welsh 52
Red Cabbage, Danish Style 79
Red Cabbage, Sweet-Sour 29
Ribs, Old-World Short 60
Rice, Baked Green 25
Rouladen with Tomato-Beer
  Kraut, Sausage-Stuffed 57
Rum, Hot Spiced Beer and 18

Salad
  Cucumber 17
  Cucumber, with Sour Cream 30
  Dressing, Beer-Oil 74
  Dressing, Poppyseed-Beer 74
  Marinated Bean 27
  Mold, Refreshing 80
  Piquant Perfection 81
  Shades o' Green 21
Salmon with Sour Cream Sauce,
  Cold 16
Sauce
  Beer Chili 22
  Beer Dessert 76
  Beer-Raisin 74
  Brown Beer 72
  Creamy Beer-Cheese 73
  Dark Caramel Beer 76
  Herbed Tomato 72

Mushroom	74
Mustard	73
Savory Barbecue	72
Sour Cream	16
Tangy Cheese	73
Sauerkraut with Apples, Lagered	80
Sausage in Beer	64
Sausage Loaf, Applesauce-Topped Beef and	61
Sausages, Cocktail Party	36
Sausage-Stuffed Rouladen with Tomato-Beer Kraut	57
Shandy Tang	93
Shellfish	
Pickled Shrimp	34
Shrimp Dunk	35
Shrimp Spread	35
Shrimp Dunk	35
Shrimp Spread	35
Shrimp, Pickled	34
Sole, Beer-Batter Fried	68
Soufflé au Bière, Cheese	51
Soufflé, Mushroom Beer	53
Soup	
Belgian Onion	45
Caraway-Cabbage	46
Cheese and Vegetable Soup with Beer	45
Corny Beef	47
Czech Beer	44
Danish Beer and Bread	44
Easy Beer-Cheese	27

Easy Franks and Bean	46
English Beer	44
Farm-Style Leek	47
Hearty Beef-Noddle	48
Hot German Beer	28
Lithuanian Beer and Poppyseed	45
Quick Canned Soup with a Zest	46
Savory Lentil	47
Seashore Beer	46
Spareribs, Savory	62
Squash and Corn, Mexican Style	25
Steak, Bachelor's	58
Steaks, Mushroom-Beer	59
Stew, Flemish Beef	56
Stew, Luxemburg	64
Stew, Savory Beef	57
Stew with Ale, Irish	20
Strata, Beery Cheese	51
Streusel, Coffeecake	38
Swedish Meatballs	17
Sweet Potatoes, Glazed	80
Syrup, Pilgrim	76
Tart, July 4th Fruit	22
Tomato Rabbit	52
Torte, Hazelnut	30
Tuna and Swiss Cheese Pie	70
Tuna-Macaroni Bake	70
Veal	
Chops, German	64

Luxemburg Stew	64
Vegetables	
Baked Green Rice	25
Beans 'n' Beer Bake	22
Beer Pilaff	79
Brussels Sprouts and Grapes	78
Chicken and Rice in Beer	67
Chili with Beer	19
Cold Potato Salad with Tart Dressing,	23
Danish Style Red Cabbage	79
French Fried Onion Rings in Beer Batter	79
German Style Green Beans	78
German Veal Chops	64
Glazed Sweet Potatoes	80
Hash Brown Potatoes	79
Hot Potato Salad	82
Lagered Sauerkraut with Apples	80
Mexican Style Pork and Beans	24
Mexican Style Squash and Corn	25
Piquant Beets	78
Sweet-Sour Red Cabbage	29
Tangy Cabbage Mold	82
Venison in Cream Gravy, Marinated	59
Waffles, Brussels	41
Wassail, Old English Hot	31
Welsh Rabbit	52
Wine, Belgian Hot Beer and	93